MISCELLANY OF THE SOUTH SEAS

MISCELLANY
of the
SOUTH SEAS

A Chinese Scholar's Chronicle of Shipwreck
and Travel through 1830s Vietnam

CAI TINGLAN *Translated and introduced*
by Kathlene Baldanza and Zhao Lu

University of Washington Press Seattle

The open access publication of *Miscellany of the South Seas* was made possible by grants from the Departments of History and Asian Studies at the Pennsylvania State University and from the Pennsylvania State University Libraries. Additional support was provided by grants from the Chiang Ching-kuo Foundation for International Scholarly Exchange and the Charles and Jane Keyes Endowment for Books on Southeast Asia.

Design by Mindy Basinger Hill
Composed in Arno Pro

UNIVERSITY OF WASHINGTON PRESS
uwapress.uw.edu

LIBRARY OF CONGRESS CONTROL NUMBER: 2023940439

ISBN 9780295751665 (hardcover)
ISBN 9780295751672 (paperback)
ISBN 9780295751689 (ebook)

♾ This paper meets the requirements
of ANSI/NISO Z39.48-1992 (Permanence of Paper)

TO CAI TINGLAN, *for living to tell the tale and for telling it so well*

Without treading the world's wild edges,

one cannot gain a full view of the world.

夫不履天下之奇險，不能得宇宙之壯觀

—*Liu Hong'ao* (*1778–1849*)

CONTENTS

ACKNOWLEDGMENTS

Cai Tinglan made friends along the way and particularly cherished those who shared his intellectual interests. We, too, cherish the friendly conversations this project has helped bring about. The Association for Asian Studies' Vietnamese Studies Group offered helpful advice, especially Li Tana, Le Thi Mai, Hoai Tran, C. Michele Thompson, and David Biggs. Li Tana offered suggestions helpful for transcribing many of the place-names. Catherine Churchman offered help and advice on transcribing Hokkien and Vietnamese words. Vũ Đường Luân guided Kate to sites in Hanoi and shared expert advice and historical references to aid our translation. Many offered suggestions, observations, and connections, including Andrew Hardy, Hue Tam Ho Tai, Sixiang Wang, Vu Duc Liem, John Phan, Nguyen Tuyet Tran, Nguyễn Tô Lan, Mike High, Thùy-Lan Đỗ, and Shuang Shen. When the COVID-19 pandemic shut down international travel, Lê Tùng Dương helped us look for traces of Cai Tinglan in the Vietnamese archives. We are grateful to Bradley Camp Davis, who read the entire manuscript and made many helpful suggestions and corrections. Ben Pease read the manuscript and made the maps. Lorri Hagman and Beth Fuget at University of Washington Press supported the project, offered feedback, and ushered it through the publication process. Cynthia Col edited the introduction and made the index. An anonymous reviewer offered pages of helpful suggestions. Nguyễn Tuấn Cường shared the manuscript copy held at Sino-Nom Research Institute and granted us permission to use it. Kate spent an enjoyable academic year at the National Humanities Center and is appreciative of the beautiful space, the intellectual community, and the good food to be found there. Kate would like to thank the many teachers and mentors who spent untold hours patiently helping her learn to read literary Chinese, including Victor Mair, Tina Lu, Paul Goldin, Liu Hsiaoping, Lin Chiufang, Fan Meeiyuan, Zhou Changzhen, Cui Yihe, and Xu Zhicheng. Michael Kulikowski, Erica Brindley and the History and Asian Studies Departments at Penn State and the Penn State University Libraries have generously supported our research, travel, and the publication of this book. Global China Studies at NYU Shanghai has also provided thoughtful support for the making of this book. And thanks to Christopher, Solomon, Lydia, and Laska—just because!

Kate Baldanza would like to particularly thank a student, a teacher, and a friend. My student Kwok-leong Tang first told me about Cai Tinglan and his adventures. Chen Yiyuan, the great Taiwanese scholar and compiler of *Hainan zazhu*, paved the way with his research and warmly welcomed our English translation. And to my dear friend Zhao Lu: finding the right words with you has been an absolute delight. Thank you for being my fellow traveler.

Speaking of traveling, Zhao Lu always believes that companionship is the best part of it. Therefore, I would like to thank Sarah Basham for her unfailing support since the conception of the project; the 2019 AAS panelists Mercedes Valmisa, Huang Wen-Yi, and Hu Xiaobai for giving us the opportunity to present the topic in an exciting framework; and my colleagues at NYU Shanghai, especially Tansen Sen, Lena Scheen, Joanna Waley-Cohen, and Zuo Lala for their embracing enthusiasm of the project. Most importantly, I would like to thank my co-author and friend Kate Baldanza for always taking me in. Besides her insightfulness and way with words, I have constantly benefitted from and been inspired by her persistence and patience, ever since we became language partners as graduate students at Penn in 2009. It has been my privilege to travel together.

INTRODUCTION

The official annals of Vietnam's Nguyễn dynasty (1802–1945) record pirate attacks, rebellion, and famine for the year 1835, as well as this minor incident:

> A merchant vessel from Fujian of the Qing headed to Taiwan on business drifted to Quảng Ngāi because of wind. Following the precedent for typhoons, the officials there gave them money and rice. Once [the officials] heard that the stipendiary student Cai Tingxiang was a passenger on the vessel, they were more solicitous and gave him an additional fifty strings of cash and twenty *fang* of rice while he waited for a convenient time to return to his country.[1]

Assisting Chinese shipwreck victims in this way was routine practice for the Nguyễn government. But for Cai Tingxiang, better known as Cai Tinglan, this was a defining episode of his life.[2] In contrast to the brief Vietnamese record, Cai wrote a much more personal account of his adventures in Nguyễn Vietnam in which he detailed his near-death experience at sea, his conversations with Vietnamese officials, and his impressions of Vietnamese society. That account, *Hainan zazhu* (Miscellany of the South Seas), is translated into English for the first time here. First published in 1837, the book offers a glimpse of Vietnamese society through the eyes of a Chinese scholar.

In 1835, Cai Tinglan was blown off course in a typhoon while sailing between Jinmen Island and the Penghu Islands in the Taiwan Strait. Cai, his brother, and their shipmates spent a harrowing week at sea before drifting to the coast of central Vietnam. After Nguyễn dynasty officials verified his self-proclaimed identity as a scholar by giving him a mock civil service examination, the Minh Mạng emperor of Vietnam permitted Cai to return to Fujian Province overland with an escort of Vietnamese soldiers. This official support allowed Cai to meet the governors-general of each province he passed through as he moved north along the imperial highway.

In the midst of his journey, which was marked by bouts of homesickness, Cai recognized the opportunity to make a name for himself at home by recording his unusual access to government officials of a foreign country. The resulting book is a rare and precious account of the social history of early nineteenth-century Vietnam. Cai Tinglan divides his tale into three chapters: a shipwreck tale, a travel diary, and an overview of Vietnamese history and culture. Cai gives vivid descriptions of clothing, food, religious practice, the day-to-day functioning of government, and other aspects of daily life. He describes the nineteenth-century view of the shallow reefs and atolls of the South China Sea (or East Sea as it is called in Vietnam) as a place to be avoided at all costs. His many encounters with Chinese overseas show the penetration of the Hokkien merchant community into Vietnamese society. His warm embrace by Nguyễn officials and his friendly "brush talks" with them demonstrate that the shared elite world of classical culture extended beyond borders.

Cai Tinglan published *Miscellany of the South Seas* to demonstrate his writing ability, Confucian forbearance, and knowledge of a foreign place in his quest to secure the holy grail of Qing literati—employment in government service. In the process, the accidental adventurer left for posterity a revealing glimpse of Vietnam in the 1830s. Once Cai's brief turn as an explorer helped him become what he had long desired to be, a scholar-official in the employ of the Qing dynasty, his book faded into obscurity.

Biography of Cai Tinglan

Cai Tinglan (1801–1859) is a celebrity in his native Penghu, also known as the Pescadores Islands, for being the only person from the islands who ever achieved imperial China's coveted palace graduate degree.[3] In some ways, he was a typical literatus who moved up the social ladder through learning and officialdom during the last imperial Chinese dynasty, the Qing dynasty (1644–1911 CE). Yet his shipwreck and journey through Vietnam distinguished him from his peers. Because of his adventure and his success in officialdom, he became the most celebrated hero of nineteenth-century Penghu.

Cai's family represented the typical trajectory from farmer to literati that often took generations. The grandfather of Cai's grandfather was a fisherman who migrated from Jinmen (then called Wuzhouyu) to the Penghu Islands in the late seventeenth century. Penghu is an archipelago located in the middle of the Taiwan Strait, between the island of Taiwan and Fujian Province (map 1). Taiwan only entered the Qing imperium in 1683, after the Qing military finally succeeded in defeating the anti-Qing resistance of the Zheng family, based in Tainan. After debate over whether the island was worth retaining, the Qing annexed it (and the Penghu Islands) as a prefecture of Fujian Province. During this period, the Chinese settlement in Taiwan and its adjacent islands increased, partially as a result of avoiding the turmoil of the Qing conquest on the mainland. But more importantly, the Penghu Islands provided not only fishing grounds but also uncultivated land for the new settlers. Taking advantage of the land, the Cai family soon moved from fishermen to well-to-do farmers. A few generations later, the Cai family could afford the schooling of Cai Tinglan's father, Cai Peihua, who became a private tutor in the Penghu area. Under Qing dynasty rule since 1727, Penghu gradually transformed from a windy, deserted island to a settled community.[4]

Cai Tinglan entered his race to officialdom like millions of other literati in late imperial China. Throughout imperial China (221 BCE–1911 CE), officialdom was the most respectable and stable career and would bring honor to an individual as well as his family. During the Qing dynasty, the only way to enter officialdom was to take the civil examinations that took place every three years. The candidates needed to pass the lowest level, the provincial examination (Ch. *xiangshi*; V. *hương*

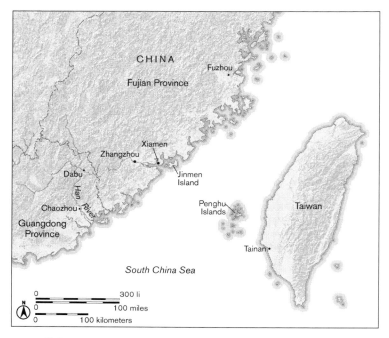

MAP 1. Fujian coast

thi) to earn the provincial graduate designation (Ch. *juren*; V. *cử nhân*; literally, "recommended man"). This title qualified them for official rank and permitted them to move to the next level, the metropolitan examination (Ch. *huishi*; V. *hội thi*), and then the palace examination (Ch. *dianshi*; V. *đình thi*). The winners of the palace exams—the palace graduates (Ch. *jinshi*; V. *tiến sĩ*; literally, "advanced scholar")—were the paramount of the literati and qualified for high-ranking positions in the Qing government. Special prestige especially went to the top three winners, namely the optimus (Ch. *zhuangyuan*; V. *trạng nguyên*), secundus (Ch. *bangyan*; V. *bảng nhãn*), and tertius (Ch. *tanhua*; V. *thản hoa*), a practice that was adopted in Vietnam only in 1843.[5] But in general, success in the civil exams elevated one's social status, allowing the fortunate few to rise from farming to the ruling elite over time.[6]

This was true for Vietnam as well. Vietnam held civil service examinations based on the Confucian classics as early as the eleventh century. During the Minh Mạng reign (1820–41), the titles and timing of the final three levels of the examinations, namely the provincial, metropolitan, and palace examinations, were brought in line with Qing dynasty practice. The bureaucratic systems of the two countries were not identical, however. As historian Alexander Woodside points out, there was a relatively higher percentage of the Vietnamese population who attained success in the examination system, and the differences between the levels of degree holders was not as stark as in China. Vietnamese licentiates were at times allowed to skip regional examinations and pass directly to the metropolitan examinations to help officials fill the Nguyễn dynasty's staffing needs.[7] Despite these and other differences, the respect afforded successful students in both China and Vietnam explains the courtesy and support Cai was shown by the Nguyễn government.

Cai Tinglan started his literati path at age five. While not from a wealthy family, he did have the advantage of being tutored by his father. This early access to learning set him ahead of his fellow villagers in marginal Penghu, a place with few educational institutions. By the age of thirteen, in 1813, he passed the prerequisite exam for the civil examinations and became a "child student" (tongsheng 童生). He then passed the prefectural licensing examination (tongshi 童試) and earned the licentiate (shengyuan 生員) title, a candidacy to take the triennial provincial exams.[8] Commonly referred to as "cultivated talent" (秀才 Ch. xiucai; V. tú tài), this title already put Cai Tinglan into the social status of the literati, for not only could the title holders enter the competition for officialdom; they also received privileges such as exemption from corvée labor. The next year, he tested first among all the child students from Taiwan Prefecture (Fu 府) and started to receive a stipend from the government.[9]

As Cai and his contemporaries knew all too well, civil examinations were a narrow path. Through the more than two hundred fifty years of the Qing dynasty, only 26,888 people were granted the palace graduate title, while the population of the dynasty peaked at 450 million during

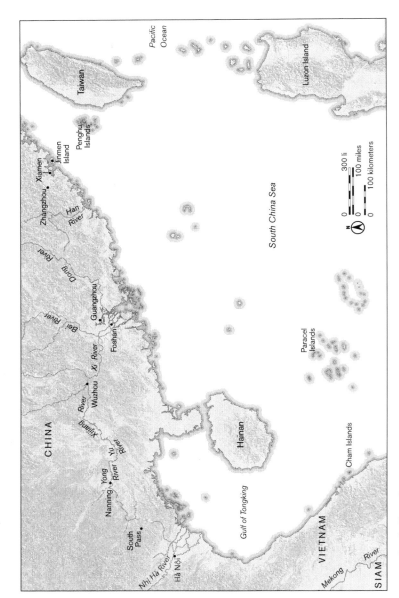

MAP 2. South China Sea

Cai's lifetime. Cai may have been a big fish in Taiwan, but he needed to go to Fujian Province, a much bigger pond, to take his provincial exams. The provincial exams in Fujian took only 50 to 140 winners every time, out of more than ten thousand examinees.[10] The format of the exam, the "eight-legged" essays (*bagu wen* 八股文), was also subject to the graders' own standards, which could be opaque to the examinees. Given the cut-throat competition, Cai repeatedly failed the provincial exams from his teenage years all the way to his mid-thirties.[11]

On November 21, 1835, while on his way back from the provincial exam in Fuzhou to the Penghu Islands, Cai Tinglan's ship encountered a typhoon.[12] His ship lost direction and drifted off the southeast coast of China and in the South China Sea for more than a week (map 2).[13] Cai and the sailors eventually reached land at the coast of Quảng Nam Province in Vietnam. Once spotted by the shore patrols of the Nguyễn, Cai and his companions needed to convince the patrol that they were not smugglers or pirates and to secure their help to return home.

Nguyễn officials, unsurprisingly, were on high alert. There are many instances of Chinese piracy recorded in *Veritable Records of the Great South* (Đại Nam thực lục), the official annals of the Nguyễn. To give some examples just from central Vietnam close in time to Cai's arrival, in 1834 two Qing pirate ships arrived in Quảng Nam, robbed merchants, and went ashore to burn down houses.[14] In 1835, a Qing pirate ship was recorded in Thới Cần, Quảng Ngãi, not long before Cai's arrival.[15] In 1836, the year after Cai Tinglan's arrival, another two Qing pirate ships were pursued and captured by the Nguyễn navy in Quảng Nam.[16] That same year, Nguyễn officials seized sixty-five *jin* of raw opium and twenty-five *liang* of refined opium from a Qing pirate ship in Quảng Ngãi.[17]

In addition to the ever-present threat of piracy and drug smuggling, the Nguyễn records show that Chinese ships did regularly drift to Vietnam after encountering storms at sea. Looking just at cases during the Minh Mạng reign involving Chinese students, there were two entries recording shipwrecked students just before Cai Tinglan's arrival. In 1822, a student from Fujian named Wang Kunyuan was blown to Vietnam while attempting to sail to Taiwan to take an examination. He was given clothing, money, and rice and allowed to return home by boat.[18] In 1831, a student of the Imperial College named Chen Qi also drifted to Vietnam.[19] This context helps us better understand Cai Tinglan's reception. The Nguyễn officials were not ready to accept Cai's explanation that he was a scholar aboard a peaceful merchant ship until the ship had been searched for contraband and Cai tested on his literary ability. Only then was Cai accepted and given extra support as a student.

After registering the ship and the personnel, Nguyễn officials made plans to return the crew to China. Cai realized that he was not completely helpless; while he could not speak Vietnamese, he could communicate with the local officials by writing in literary Chinese, a common method among the literati of East Asian countries in the late imperial period. According to Vietnamese law, Cai's cultivated talent title distinguished him from the rest of the people on the ship. Given that Vietnam under the Nguyễn dynasty also administered civil service examinations, it recognized and respected Cai's degree. He was further invited to meet with the provincial administration commissioner, Nguyễn Bạch, who bonded with Cai through their shared Confucian literati identity. In this foreign land, Cai found a familiar role to play.

Cai's Qing literati identity opened the path back to China. Faced with the frequent piracy and smuggling, Nguyễn Bạch initially seemed to have had doubts about Cai's self-proclaimed identity as a literatus. After the meeting, he sent a few civil-examination questions to Cai, asking him to finish by the next day. Cai passed the bar; after a few days, local provincial officials began to visit and socialize with this literatus from the Heavenly Court (Ch. Tianchao; V. Thiên Triều). According to Cai's account, on December 24, 1835, the Vietnamese emperor Minh Mạng issued an edict that recognized Cai's literatus status and accommodated him and his companions with money and rice. The recognition from the emperor opened a path of official support for Cai.

With the support of the Nguyễn government assured, the next question was how to get back home. According to Vietnamese law, Vietnamese officials needed to escort Chinese literati by the sea route, and only merchants and commoners were allowed to take the land route. The law was meant to privilege the literati; the sea route was not only much faster but also avoided bandits, onerous paperwork, and other logistics required for land travel. However, Cai insisted on returning by land; otherwise, he would have had to wait until favorable currents the next spring. Also, after experiencing the trauma of being lost at sea, it is possible that he was not ready to again set foot onboard a ship (see Cai's travel route on maps 3A and 3B). The Vietnamese officials were hesitant to grant permission, given that the overland route was both more dangerous and more expensive—and they would bear responsibility. But eventually, they received permission directly from the emperor.

The next obstacle was money. In addition to paperwork for local authorities, traveling required food and lodging. Since Cai's intended route from Fuzhou to Penghu was short, he had neither sufficient money for a months-long trip nor goods to trade. Even if he had money, it would still be difficult to find lodging in small villages or deserted areas. In a land where he could not even speak the language, Cai found himself in a predicament.

But once again, a solution emerged. China and Vietnam had long had trading relations, and since the seventeenth century, Chinese merchants from Fujian and Guangdong Provinces had traveled and migrated to Vietnam in large numbers.[20] By 1835, they had formed communities recognized by the Vietnamese government, called "associations" (Ch., V. *bang*). After meeting with the Quảng Ngãi magistrate, Cai was introduced to the head of the Fujian Association, Teng Kim, who provided him a place to stay. Even though he was from Penghu, Cai was perceived as part of the wider Fujianese circle. He was glad to be seen this way; during his trip back to Fujian, he stayed with and was accompanied mostly by speakers of Hokkien, the language of southeastern Fujian. Among the Chinese immigrants who paid visits to Cai, Cai identified most with people from Fujian, who shared daily customs and native language. Cai found a community in a foreign land.

Logistical problems solved, Cai was on his way to China on January 9, 1836. By June 21 that year, he was back in his mother's house in

CHINA

Qian River

Pingnan · Wuzho

Xunzhou ·

Xun River

Yongchun
county
seat

Gui
county
seat

Yu River

Nanning ·

Yong River

Hengzhou

· Taipingzhen

Shangshi · Ningming
South ·
Pass · Lang Sơn

Nhi Hà River

Lang Giang

Hà Nội · · Bắc Ninh

Thường Tín

Lý Nhân ·

Ninh Bình

Thanh Hóa ·

Gulf of Tongking

VIETNAM

Hainan

· Nghệ An

· Hà Tĩnh
· Hà Hoa
—Transverse Mountain Pass

"Chợ Ròn" ·
"Chợ Luân" ·
Đồng Hới ·
Quang Bình
Province

South China Sea

Quảng Trị ·
Phú Xuân ·

Ocean Mountain Pass

Marble Mountains · · Cham Islands
· Hội An
Quảng Nam
Province · Sa Cần estuary of Trà Bồng River

· Quảng Ngãi or "Cù Mông"

Paracel
Islands

Mekong River

SIAM

continues on next map

N

0		300 li
0		100 mile
0		100 kilometers

MAP 3A. Route from Vietnam to China

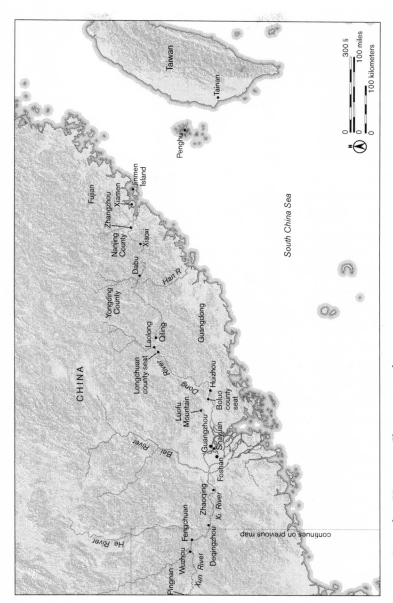

MAP 3B. Route from Vietnam to China, continued

Penghu. During these five months, he became adept at traveling in Vietnam without knowing the language. Whenever he reached a new town, he went to the local magistrate's office to present his documents and his status as a Chinese literatus. This combination guaranteed that he would be welcomed by the local officials. Cai consistently reported that he was invited to feast with the officials and exchange poetry. Subsequently, he had no problem with the paperwork required to pass provincial borders or, later, the Chinese border. When it came to daily accommodation, his Fujianese identity allowed him to seek and receive help from his fellow Fujianese. Meanwhile, he received food, medicine, and money from other Qing Chinese migrants because they were all "people of the Tang" (Ch. Tangren; V. Đường nhân).

Once he was back in Fujian, Cai decided to capitalize on his accident and turned to his mentor, Zhou Kai (1779–1837), for help. Zhou, the provincial magistrate in Fujian, provided critical support for his student. Previously, in 1832, when Zhou was the circuit intendant of Quanzhou, Cai had contacted him regarding the current famine in Penghu to request aid for the island. Zhou had been impressed not only by Cai's proposal of distributing financial aid but also by his talent in composing poetry. Eventually, he decided to take Cai under his wing, even giving the latter a new style name, Xiangzu (Source of Fragrance). In the next few years, Cai confided his anxiety about passing the civil examinations to Zhou; in response, Zhou comforted him with poetry.

When Cai returned to China, he saw Zhou Kai first in Xiamen (Amoy) on June 5 of 1836, even before seeing his mother. He told Zhou about his adventure, and the latter thought he had been "reborn." When Cai wrote *Miscellany of the South Seas* to recount his travels, Zhou contributed a preface in which he describes Cai's triumph over the obstacles strewn in his way as a testament to his filial piety and composure. If Cai could survive the unprecedented heaven-sent difficulties of his sojourn in Vietnam, Zhou suggested, he could certainly handle anything that came his way at court. Zhou's advocacy promoted Cai among the literati circles in Taiwan. One year later, Zhou became the circuit intendant of Taiwan and immediately appointed Cai as the main lecturer at the Chongwen Academy and two other academies. Although he still lacked an advanced degree at this time, Cai was well respected thanks to the endorsement and support of Zhou Kai.

Cai had his break in 1844. That year, he finally passed the provincial exam and earned a palace graduate degree. In the same year, he was appointed to be a magistrate in Jiangxi. Five years later, he was assigned to Xiajiang County in Jiangxi. During his tenure, he promoted education and reduced taxes for this impoverished county. Soon after, in 1852, he became the examiner of Jiangxi and the associate administrator in charge of water conservancy. In 1856, he was moved to nearby Fengcheng County and earned praise for his work on flood control. It was there that he passed away in 1859. Cai had fulfilled the dream of many to become a literatus-official.

Given that *Miscellany of the South Seas* fell into obscurity fairly quickly, we cannot say with any certainty whether it helped Cai Tinglan make connections or climb the career ladder. We can see from the forewords that his friends presented his handling of himself abroad and the knowledge he gained through his travels as an asset. Cai Tinglan himself may have seen his book as a professional calling card, demonstrating his calm under pressure and his literary ability. There is a venerable history of Chinese scholars writing about the exotic south to show off their literary prowess, unusual experiences, and masculinity. The authors Liu Zongyuan (773–819), Su Shi (1037–1101), Fan Chengda (1126–1193), Xu Xiake (1587–1641), and Kuang Lu (1604–1650) all fit this mold.[21] While Cai Tinglan, like these authors, constructed a self through travel narrative, it is notable that he did not exoticize Vietnam to create a more colorful backdrop for his exploits.

Publication and Translation History of *Miscellany of the South Seas*

Cai Tinglan published his account of his journey very soon after his return to China. Both the first and second printing of the first edition came out in 1837.[22] In the rush to publish, Cai left out his poems, writing,

"The poetry will later appear in the last chapter." In the second printing, this line was changed to "Yuyuan's [Cai's art name] personal blocks," suggesting that Cai owned the blocks carved with the poems and was perhaps intending to save them or print them separately. These poems were apparently never published and have not been preserved, nor have they appeared in any Vietnamese collections. Given the importance of poetry in his communication with Vietnamese officials, it is unfortunate that they have not survived.

A second edition soon followed the first. It was printed in two runs, with some minor changes to the text. The surviving copies of the second printing are not complete. Of these four versions of the text, the National Library in Beijing has two original copies, and the National Library in Taipei has one.[23]

A handwritten copy of the first edition preserved at the Institute of Sino-Nom Studies (Viện Nghiên cứu Hán Nôm) in Hà Nội (shelf number HVv.80) forms the base text for our translation. We have also consulted other editions of this text and note substantial differences in the footnotes. The differences between the first and second editions of *Miscellany of the South Seas* are minor but telling. Cai revised some sentences that described Vietnamese people reacting to his appearance with surprise, awe, or even mirth. In the revision, he modestly shifts the focus away from himself and also away from any perceived slight to Qing dignity. In the earlier edition, Cai explicitly explains that he was wearing formal clothes, and we know, too, that he would have been wearing the queue hairstyle of shaved forehead and long ponytail required by the Qing government of all men. While common people gawked and laughed at the sight of a queue-wearing foreigner in formal clothes, treating Cai as a figure of merriment, Vietnamese officials tempered their initial surprise at Cai's appearance with polite welcome. The awkwardness and friction of these initial accounts are edited out of the second edition. These changes also present the Vietnamese common people in a less unflattering light.

After this initial publication flurry, interest in the book among Chinese readers appears to have faded. Having achieved his goal of attaining the palace graduate title and a position in officialdom, Cai Tinglan no longer needed to promote the book. Although *Miscellany of the South Seas* fell out of view in China, it was translated into Russian in 1877. In 1878, it was translated from Russian into French.[24] It is no surprise that it attracted the attention of a French-speaking audience, given that country's ongoing piecemeal colonization of what became known as Indochina and concomitant interest in information about Vietnam.

Miscellany of the South Seas was not reprinted again until 1959. At that time, a Taiwanese version based on the incomplete and poorly printed copy of the second edition held by the National Library in Taipei was published.[25] In 2006, the Taiwanese scholar Chen Yiyuan compiled and introduced Cai Tinglan's work under the title *Cai Tinglan and His Miscellany of the South Seas* (Cai Tinglan jiqi Hainan zazhu). A Vietnamese translation of Professor Chen's book by Ngô Đức Thọ and Hoàng Văn Lâu appeared as *Thái Đình Lan và tác phẩm Hải Nam Tạp Trứ* in 2009. Gotō Hitoshi (後藤均) led a reading group that made a partial translation of *Miscellany of the South Seas* into Japanese in 1992.[26] A Korean translation is in the works, part of the trend of recent interest in the text across East Asia. In addition, the text is digitized and available online on the website of the Chinese Text Project.[27]

Cai Tinglan has consistently received scholarly attention in Taiwan, as an illustrious representative of Taiwan and as the only person from Penghu to ever receive a palace graduate degree. His house in Penghu has been preserved as a museum (Cai Tinglan Jinshi Di 蔡廷蘭進士第).

Navigating the South China Sea in the Age of Sail

Cai Tinglan boarded a boat in Jinmen, an island off the coast of Fujian, bound for his home in the Penghu Islands. The Fujianese sailors were well aware of various hazards in the vicinity, but once they were blown off course, they could not judge where they were in relation to these obstacles. Although farther away, drifting to Luzon (Manila) in the Philippine Islands or to Siam (modern-day Thailand) was preferred, because it would be straightforward to sail back home to Fujian from those locations. The large Chinese merchant communities in either place could provide material support for the return of their compatriots. More concerning would be to crash on the rocky atolls that studded the shallow waters of the South China Sea. Their fears first turned to the notorious Nan'aoqi.

The 1730 text *Record of Things Heard and Seen in the Maritime Kingdoms* (*Haiguo wenjian lu*) by Chen Lunjiong gives the following account of the southeastern coast of Nan'ao Island, off the coast of Guangdong:

> Nan'aoqi is located on the southeast coast of Nan'ao [island].
> There are islets that are small and low-lying, with feet extending
> out from all sides made of vegetation-covered stones. Long sea
> plants extend from the seafloor. There are sandbars in the bay
> that suck in anything that drifts by; boats should not go there.
> Once you enter the current then you get sucked to that place
> and cannot get out. About seven watches away from Nan'ao
> by the sea route is what has been called since ancient times
> "entering the current" [*luoji*]. The north is bounded by sunken
> and raised sand for about 200 *li*, about three watches by the sea
> route."[28]

Their next concerns were the One Thousand *Li* Stone Embankment (Ch. Qianlishitang; V. Thiên Lý Thạch Đường) and the Ten Thousand *Li* Sandy Shoal (Ch. Wanlichangsha; V. Vạn Lý Trường Sa) Islands. In common use at that time, these terms generally described the treacherously shallow waters in the middle of the South China Sea. Alternatively, these two place-names are sometimes associated with the modern-day names Paracel Islands and Spratly Islands. Mariners would either hug the coast or travel on known routes with deeper water to avoid running aground far from inhabited land.

European and American mariners were no strangers to these dangerous waters. John White, a lieutenant in the United States Navy, wrote in his 1823 account of a voyage to Vietnam that they avoided "the group of islands and shoals called the Paracels":

The Paracels, just mentioned, were formerly, and indeed till very recently, dreaded by navigators, being represented as one continuous chain of low islands, coral reefs, and sandbanks, extending from the latitude of 12° to that of 17° north, in a north-north-east and south-south-west direction, forming a fancied resemblance to a human foot (the toe of which was the southernmost extremity). . . . This archipelago, once so formidable from its great imaginary extent, is now ascertained to be a group of islands and reefs, of no great extent, with good and safe channels between most of them, and in many places good anchorage.[29]

They relied on the charts made in 1818 by Ross and Maughan of the Bombay Marine of the "different passages leading to the Macau roads."

What is clear throughout Cai Tinglan's account is the close connection between Fujian and central Vietnam. The Tongking Gulf (or Tonkin Gulf) forms its own distinct and cohesive region spanning the political boundary of China and Vietnam, but the Leizhou peninsula, Hainan Island, and the peak-studded inlets of the gulf tend to serve as a barrier between areas of China to the north and areas of Vietnam to the south.[30] Historian Charles Wheeler labels this zone connected by water the Tongking Stream, which was plied by coastal ships traveling to the west of Hainan Island and was dotted by coves and islands that made it an ideal lair for pirates.[31] This contrasts with the Fujian Stream, which connected Fujian and central Vietnam, bypassing the Tongking Gulf. Thus, somewhat surprisingly, there were strong ties between Fujian and central Vietnam. Despite the distance, these regions were connected by water. As a case in point, Cai Tinglan encountered three Vietnamese officials who had traveled to Xiamen, compared with two who had traveled to the capital, Beijing.

Cai mentions the "inner sea" and the "outer sea." Historian Ronald Po defines the Qing understanding of these two zones: "The inner sea constituted the empire's domestic seawater. . . . By contrast, the outer sea was a capricious domain that lay beyond the purview of administrative governance and economic extraction."[32] The line between these two sea spaces was situational. While Po's definition is based on the Qing's division of political space, Cai sees them through the eyes of a sailor; to him, these terms define spaces of relative safety and danger. Cai views the outer sea as the space just beyond the coast out of sight of the shore where navigation becomes more complicated and the danger of storms increases. Once his ship entered the Blackwater Ocean, it was off course. Fang Junshi in *General Record of the Ocean* (Haiyang jilüe) describes the Blackwater Ocean as off the coast of Guangdong and "beyond our [Qing] governance and control."[33]

Chinese Overseas in Eighteenth- and Nineteenth-Century Vietnam

Nguyễn Vietnam was newly consolidated, expansive, and plugged into interregional trade networks, and it claimed rulership over diverse populations. Cai Tinglan arrived in Vietnam during the fourth decade of the dynasty under its second ruler, Minh Mạng. The founding emperor of the Nguyễn, the Gia Long emperor, was descended from the Nguyễn ruling family that had once controlled the south (the Cochinchina of European records, known as Đàng Trong or the "inner region" in Vietnamese) before being driven away by the Tây Sơn (1778–1802). The Nguyễn dynasty claimed to be the legitimate successors of the previous Lê dynasty (1428–1789) of imperial Vietnam, but much was new in the nineteenth century. Perhaps most notably, the territory under Vietnamese imperial control was much larger than in any previous period, stretching from the Red River delta in the north to the Mekong delta in the far south. The Gia Long emperor built his capital in the center of the territory, in Huế, near his family's former seat, moving Vietnamese political power away from its historical center in Hà Nội. The Nguyễn state sought to incorporate diverse groups of people into its state, from non-Vietnamese peoples in the highlands, Chams in central and southern Vietnam, and Chinese communities centered on far-flung entrepôts, especially in central and southern Vietnam. The country formerly known as Đại Việt also had a new name: Việt Nam (or Vietnam). This is the name used by Cai Tinglan through his text.

Much would have looked familiar to Cai. All government work was conducted in literary Chinese, moving away from the Vietnamese demotic script, chữ Nôm, that had been favored during the Tây Sơn period. The main divisions of government—six ministries run by bureaucrats chosen through a civil service examination and presided over by the emperor, as well as government sponsorship of Confucianism—was broadly the same as in Qing China.[34] Vietnamese dynasties had long held civil service examinations to recruit erudite men for government careers. The palace examination was halted during the reign of the Gia Long emperor, who wished to calm north-south tensions and knew the bulk of the degrees would go to northern scholars.[35] His successor, the Minh Mạng emperor, reinstated the national-level competition in 1822 and held them every three years. Cai Tinglan made a point of recording his meetings with several Vietnamese palace graduates.

Although Cai and his shipmates were disoriented and frightened while lost at sea, they were in fact following a well-traveled current that connected Fujian to Vietnam's central coast. The Fujian Stream, frequented by oceangoing vessels that skirted the dangerous Paracel Islands, connected central Vietnam to Fujian and northward to Japanese and Korean ports. The currents that connected distant Fujian to central Vietnam had long carried people, commodities, capital, and ideas between the two places. Fujianese merchants had been active in Vietnam since at least the Song dynasty (960–1279). Even before the fall of the Ming, Chinese traders were drawn to the lucrative markets of what is now southern Vietnam, especially following the partial lifting of the sea ban in 1567.[36] Following the fall of the Ming dynasty in the mid-seventeenth century, Ming refugees flowed into Southeast Asia seeking to settle beyond Qing control, becoming the "Minh Hương," the majority of whom had roots in Fujian Province. Minh Hương literally means "Ming incense," indicating people who continued to offer sacrifices to the Ming dynasty—in other words, Ming loyalists. Despite the name, rather than as a political group looking for an opportunity to restore a fallen dynasty, the Minh Hương are better understood as emigrants who were both pushed out of China due to instability and policy changes under the Qing and drawn by the pull of opportunity in what is now Vietnam. They planned to make Vietnam a permanent home, not necessarily a base for military action against the Qing. The Minh Hương were given special privileges by the Nguyễn lords of Cochinchina, predecessors of the Nguyễn dynasty encountered by Cai. They were allowed to intermarry with Vietnamese, own land, conduct trade, and govern their own communities. They came to serve as "seatrade brokers, royal bureaucrats, and cultural intermediaries."[37] Just as merchants used their wealth and social status to enter the literati class through education and marriage ties, Chinese merchant emigrants in Vietnam used the same strategies to become a minority elite.[38]

While fighting Ming loyalist forces in Taiwan between 1664 and 1683, the Qing forced an evacuation of the southeast coast and a ban on maritime activities, devastating the coastal economy. Recovery was slow throughout the eighteenth century, as bans on sojourning overseas enacted early in the century continued to stymie trading families and push some of their activities underground. The relaxing of Qing maritime trade bans in 1754 ushered in a "Chinese century" during which miners, traders, adventurers, and entrepreneurs of all kinds sought economic opportunities across Southeast Asia. The Nguyễn royal family of Vietnam made use of the Chinese community to expand their control of the hinterlands and increase their tax base.[39]

In the mid-eighteenth century, Fujianese and Cantonese trade with Southeast Asia increased rapidly. This period was also the peak of migration of Chinese settlers into the region. These "Chinese" settlers were in no way monolithic; dialect and place of origin created very real divisions. Struggles between Chaozhou (or, as it is sometimes transliterated to reflect local pronunciation, Teochew) and Cantonese communities influenced political formations in the "water frontier" stretching from Saigon to Bangkok. Indeed, when Cai Tinglan mentions Chaozhou, although technically located in Guangdong Province, he treats it as a part of the larger Hokkien world. This is understandable, as the Chaozhou dialect (or Teochew/Hoklo) is a southern Min language closely related to Hokkien; Chaozhou and southern Fujian formed a connected culture, despite their locations in different provinces. Fujianese traders occupied a different plane, having arrived earlier, dominating the circle of wealthy merchants, intermarrying with elite Vietnamese families, and producing children who went on to occupy important posts in the Nguyễn government.[40] Chinese merchants had a high status and political role in Đàng Trong.[41]

Minh Hương and more recently arrived Qing Chinese were clearly separated from one another. Qing Chinese were also known colloquially as Tang people (V. Đường Nhân), referring to the Tang dynasty (618–907 CE); however, this designation is cultural, not temporal. Tang people meant people from China, often southern regions, but not Chinese communities established since the Tang. Somewhat counterintuitively, Tang people were more recent arrivals than Minh Hương. Cai Tinglan used neither "Minh Hương" nor references to the Qing dynasty, such as "Qing people" in his account. Instead, he used "Tang people" or the strikingly modern-sounding "Chinese people" (Ch. Zhongguoren). Cai explains that "in Annam, Chinese people are called Tang people" and also call themselves Tang people, suggesting that the terms Tang person and Chinese person were nearly interchangeable. Later in the text, he states that Chinese people are also called "people of the Heavenly Court" (Ch. Tianchaoren). Cai seems to use "Tang people" to refer to more established communities of Chinese, and "Chinese people" to refer to sojourners or temporary residents. We have translated the terms as Chinese and Tang people in order to make the differentiation in the original clear. When Cai writes about named individuals, he simply provides their province and county of origin.

Qing Chinese were at least initially identifiable by the Qing-mandated queue hairstyle—a shaved forehead and long ponytail (as Cai observes in his account). Sojourners rather than emigrants, many Qing people intended to make money abroad and eventually return to China. In practice, some Qing people could not afford to return, and others did not wish to. Still others may have stayed longer than they intended or found ways to move back and forth between the two countries. Qing people also established families in Vietnam. Sojourning could be a prelude to migration.[42]

In 1814, the Gia Long emperor decreed that overseas Chinese could divide into native-place associations (*bang*) for self-government, with a group leader (*bang trưởng*) responsible for relaying government decrees, collecting taxes within the group, and generally managing the affairs of the group.[43] The seven associations recognized in 1814 were the Guangzhao (Guangzhou and Zhaoqing), Fujian, Chaozhou, Fuzhou, Kejia (Hakka), Hainan, and Qiongzhou associations.[44] This division was based not only on province but also on ethnicity and language, especially Hokkien, Cantonese, and Hakka.[45] Later in the dynasty, the Nguyễn designated more groups and attempted to absorb the powerful Minh Hương into the associations.[46] Chinese overseas communities, even before this decree, were organized around native-place associations.

What services did native-place associations provide? They were social clubs and hostels; they housed shrines to regional deities; they would ensure the burial or shipment of remains home when compatriots died abroad; and they helped new arrivals get oriented, join a network of compatriots, and establish a base from which to make connections beyond their association.[47] Cai Tinglan stayed at the Fujian native-place lodge in Hà Nội, which is still located on Lãn Ông Street in the Old Quarter and is currently used as a school.[48] The native-place associations were a resource for the Chinese, but they were also encouraged by the Vietnamese government as a way to keep track of this mobile population.

Under the reigns of Minh Mạng and Triệu Trị (r. 1841–47), these policies shifted toward actively encouraging assimilation in order to decrease the power of Minh Hương communities. In 1827, the characters used to represent Minh Hương were changed from "incense" to "village" (香 to 鄉, both pronounced *xiang* in Modern Standard Mandarin), diluting the political loyalism suggested by the name. The Minh

Mạng emperor forbade Minh Hương from "returning" to China with their Vietnamese wives or children or from wearing Qing dress. At the same time, he preserved their existing legal rights and re-affirmed their responsibilities, including providing translation services and regulating prices and coinage in the markets.[49]

By the time Cai arrived in the early nineteenth century, the overseas Chinese community was imbricated in Vietnam's commercial, institutional, and social life. He frequently encountered the native-place associations and received help from them, especially the Fujian Association. Many of his elite interlocutors informed him that their ancestors had originated in Fujian. At the same time, newer Qing arrivals kept connections between China and Vietnam strong, even as some of the older traditions faded. For instance, some earlier community centers of Minh Hương likely lost relevance as they assimilated more deeply into Vietnamese society. Describing Hội An (Faifo), "where Chinese people were most numerous," Cai writes:

> There was an old transshipment depot which was really spacious. (Inside they offer sacrifice to every commissioner from the previous dynasty, but Chinese people do not maintain the sacrifice well. Now it has returned to local people's protection. It is often blocked off, and people are not allowed to go in.)

Hội An, once the most important trade port on Vietnam's central coast, was partially destroyed during the Tây Sơn uprising in the late eighteenth century. It continued to lose relevance as the Thu Bồn river silted up and other ports, especially Saigon, grew in importance.

Scholars of the overseas Chinese have long been making the case that the history of China cannot be fully understood without incorporating an understanding of the influence of expatriate Chinese communities. Most of these emigrants traveled to Southeast Asia. In general, they did not view their physical separation from China as a permanent severing of ties with the Chinese world. Rather, they were expanding that world. In fact, emigration can be seen as a form of overseas expansion.[50] Viewed in this light, nodes of central Vietnam appear as both Vietnamese sovereign territory and as a Fujianese hinterland. As historian Melissa Macauley observes in the context of the South China Sea, "'periphery' and 'core' or 'metropole' and 'hinterland,' or even 'colonizer' and 'colonized,' were complicated and fungible."[51] On Chaozhou's entanglement with Southeast Asian polities, she writes, "In this entangled relationship, there was neither metropole nor hinterland but an increasingly interrelated trans-local economy that was dominated by Chinese, often at the invitation of colonizer, monarchs, and sultans."[52]

Macauley's work on maritime Chaozhou pushes back against the "ecological cul-de-sac" argument famously made by historian Kenneth Pomeranz to partially explain "the great divergence" between Chinese and British industrialization and modernization.[53] While British industrialization was fueled by access to the resources of overseas colonies, the theory goes, China was running short of resources with no access to overseas colonies. Macauley suggests instead that Chinese maritime settlements functioned like colonies; they allowed for resource extraction, investment opportunities, and jobs to absorb excess workers who in turn sent sizable remittances to their native places. Unlike European colonialism, Chinese settlements in Southeast Asia operated without military or political support from the Qing government. As such, they have been less visible to historians than traditional European colonies. Moreover, this form of colonialism was cheaper and more effective than the Euro-American version. Perhaps, as Macauley suggests, it is better described as a non-statist form of territoriality, whereby Chinese merchants had access to markets and natural resources and engaged in commerce in a way that maximized group benefits.[54]

Much of Macauley's work focuses on Siam and the Straits Settlements of British Malaya, where many Chaozhouese settled. As she demonstrates, the British created a colonial society in which Chinese traders reaped great profits, deepening British dependence on Chinese capital, labor, and trading networks. The political situation in Nguyễn dynasty Vietnam was different. The Nguyễn dynasty, too, profited from and made use of the Chinese population and their trade networks, while perhaps achieving more success at monitoring that community. Native-place associations not only facilitated networking opportunities for Chinese emigrants, they also helped the Nguyễn dynasty organize and keep tabs on Chinese emigrants in their territory. Chinese trading networks and tax farming contributed to the Nguyễn economy. Chinese trade to southern Vietnam was largely unidirectional. Vietnamese and Chinese merchants took up their roles in interlocking interregional trade networks by tacit agreement. Chinese merchants brought Chinese goods along the long-distance route into central Vietnamese ports and purchased Vietnamese goods to sell at home. Vietnamese traders engaged in riverine trade and short-distance coastal trade along the Gulf of Siam.[55] European and American representatives eager to establish trading depots in Vietnam were baffled by this situation. When Vietnamese rulers repeatedly rebuffed their requests, they mistakenly assumed that the Qing government controlled Vietnam and sought to preserve their trading dominance. In fact, the trading system worked well for the Nguyễn, and they had no wish to destabilize it by granting Europeans and Americans more access.

The Nguyễn government's relatively strong control of its coast suggests that Vietnam, at least, was not a Chinese "colony" or territory in the way Macauley describes for other Southeast Asian locations. Southern Vietnam was an international crossroads of goods and people, where cultures and languages mixed in busy ports and markets. Traditionally understood as "merchants without empire," new research is revisiting the role of the Qing empire in overseas Chinese communities.[56] It may be that the Qing government was more in contact with and invested in overseas Chinese communities than has been previously acknowledged; one example is Hà Tiên, a trading enclave on Vietnam's southern coast, whose leaders are sometimes described as Ming loyalists.[57] This dynamic applies to China as well. The internal migration of Cantonese within China may have been just as important to the construction of empire as sedentary, registered people farming a single crop. Furthermore, the distinction between sojourners and settlers is fluid, as one can seamlessly shift to the other.[58] On the one hand, the mobility and transnational connections of Chinese merchants reveal a world of activity not under the full control of the Qing government. On the other hand, imported rice was critically important to Qing China, and the government at times accepted the economic dependence of coastal Guangdong and Fujian on Southeast Asia sojourning and trade. The Qing was a great naval power that proactively integrated its empire with the maritime world through "maritime militarization and seaborne shipping" in the long eighteenth century.[59] Central and southern Vietnam can be considered as interconnected with maritime Chaozhou, a region that stretched beyond Chaozhou north to Shanghai and south to along the Gulf of Siam.[60] The significance of *Miscellany of the South Seas* is that it shows us precisely how these linkages worked in practice.

Multilingualism and the Two Worlds of *Miscellany of the South Seas*

Despite being in a foreign land, Cai Tinglan was surprised to discover that he had not strayed beyond the extended water world of southeastern China. Although Cai initially felt lost and adrift while abroad, he discovered that he was passing through a well-established trade corridor that had long shuttled people and products between the southeastern coast of China and the central coast of Vietnam. Cai found that he could move easily in two linguistic registers: the elite register of literary Chinese unlocked through learned "brush talks" and the Hokkien-speaking register of diasporic Fujianese traders. Cai Tinglan was able to leverage his double identity as a Hokkien speaker and a scholar to move with ease through Nguyễn Vietnam. Cai Tinglan simultaneously traveled through a Hokkien-speaking Fujianese maritime world and a cosmopolitan ecumene that communicated in literary Chinese poetry filled with scholarly allusions. His trip profoundly reveals the multilingual nature of the social worlds of Nguyễn Vietnam and Qing China.

When Cai communicates with the sailors aboard his ship and the overseas Chinese community, he presents himself as a Fujianese native. Like his compatriots among the emigrant community, his local place affiliations were more primary than his identification with the Qing or China as a whole. The Vietnamese government relied on the large and well-connected community of Fujianese to serve as translators and hosts for Cai Tinglan and his brother. Moved by their shared home-place, Fujianese people offered Cai and his brother monetary support at several points in their journey. As he moves north and passes out of the Fujianese Stream and into the Tongking Stream, Cai encounters fewer Fujianese and more compatriots from Guangdong.

When he engaged with Vietnamese officials, Cai presented himself as a scholar from the Heavenly Court, signaling to them that he was a member of their elite community and that he shared their cosmopolitan code. This transnational cultural world has been labeled in various ways. Historian of China and Vietnam Alexander Woodside dubbed it a "Confucian commonwealth" whose members recognized themselves as part of an intellectual community that extended beyond political boundaries with deep roots in past tradition.[61] In literary studies, scholars have championed terms such as the "Sinophographic cosmopolis," a reworking of Sheldon Pollock's "Sanskrit Cosmopolis."[62] The linguistic "Sinosphere" or character-based "Sinographosphere" each aim to cover places that were influenced by literary Chinese, even if the inhabitants do not speak a Sinophone language.[63] James Millward, noting that the "Chinese cultural ecumene" bears striking similarities to the Greco-Roman linguistic and cultural tradition of Europe and the Mediterranean or to the Persian-language Islamic tradition of North Africa and Asia, dubs it a "Sinicate."[64] Whatever the label, this cultural world cuts against narratives of a unitary China bound by its territorial borders. More than an academic theory, this cosmopolitan community structured interactions across an enormous geographic expanse in the early modern world. When Cai Tinglan was blown off course, we know he was still within this familiar territory when, arriving in an unknown port, a man in a boat, unable to communicate in a shared spoken language, traces the two characters 安南 (Annan or Annam) with his finger.

The two worlds—that of the Fujianese diaspora and the Confucian commonwealth—interpenetrated. One of Cai Tinglan's most illustrious interlocutors, Phan Thanh Giản, was the grandson of a Minh Hương from southern Fujian. Other officials throughout the narrative mention their Chinese family origins. Although his Hokkien-speaking guides did not necessarily know literary Chinese or converse with Nguyễn officials, the Fujian community was called upon by the Nguyễn government at several points to provide services (food, lodging, and translation) to Cai and his brother.

The crew of Cai's ship was initially held in suspicion by local officials. This only cleared once the ship was searched for contraband (drugs and weapons) and Cai demonstrated that he was truly a scholar by taking a written exam. Piracy was a problem for the Nguyễn government at this time and place. In addition to a steady stream of European and American ships demanding unrealistic trading privileges and Asian pirates engaging in smuggling, the Nguyễn government was still engaged in putting down the Saigon-based Lê Văn Khôi revolt (1833–35). The Nguyễn would remember that the Tây Sơn deployed Qing pirates to fight the Nguyễn royal family in their long quest to regain control of Vietnam, sometimes called the Thirty Years War. It was also a time when the Minh Mạng emperor was working to limit the role of Chinese traders within the country and close loopholes that allowed them to evade taxation or smuggle Vietnamese rice into China.[65] Chinese traders found ways to evade new restrictions, and it had happened that traders pretended they had been blown off course and then engaged in illicit trade while waiting to return to China.[66] Once their story of being blown off course by a typhoon was verified, the Nguyễn government granted permission for the sailors to wait in Vietnam until the monsoon season passed and then to return home by boat. Ultimately, Cai Tinglan's double identity as a Hokkienese and a scholar secured him safe harbor and a warm welcome across Vietnam.

Due to their geographical and historical adjacency, people in Penghu, Jinmen, and Tong'an spoke a particular dialect of Hokkien, the Quanzhou dialect of the Quanzhang division.[67] Growing up in Penghu, Cai spoke this dialect. Meanwhile, a common tongue, or "official language" (*guanhua*), the predecessor to today's Mandarin, was used in late imperial China, especially among the officials and the literati. As a government-sponsored student, he was probably able to speak in some version of this common tongue, besides being well versed in literary Chinese writing. During his trip in Vietnam, he received help from people who could speak "Chinese speech" (Huayu) as well as "Min tongue" (Minyin), showing the division between Mandarin and Hokkien.

Cai's experiences tapped into a larger multilinguistic situation among the Chinese emigrants in Vietnam. Cai relied on communication in Hokkien, especially the Quanzhou dialect. Of the thirteen people who hosted him, twelve came from Hokkien-speaking regions. Among the twelve hosts, five were from the Quanzhou dialect region Tong'an or Jinjiang; three were from Longxi or Zhao'an, two regions where the Zhangzhou dialect of the Quanzhang division was spoken; two were from the Chaoshan division of the Hokkien-speaking region Chaozhou of Guangdong; and only one was from Taiping in Guangxi, a Cantonese speaking region.[68] Cai used Hokkien daily while in Vietnam. This was particularly the case when it involved intimate interactions, such as staying as a guest at someone's house. In contrast, Mandarin did not have much space in this sector.

Nonetheless, the "official language," or certain types of nineteenth-century Mandarin, could be used on other occasions. By the first decades of the nineteenth century, a Nanjing-based Mandarin dialect dominated as the Mandarin koine among the literati and the officials. Later in the century, the Beijing-based dialect of Mandarin started to gain more prestige. People in Qing China then, especially the literati, could communicate across linguistic groups with a Nanjing or Beijing dialect of Mandarin, or more practically, a hybrid of both.[69] For example, when the shipwreck brought him into Vietnamese territory, a "Chinese" (Huayu)-speaking person approached Cai and the sailors, asking about their identity. During Cai's trip in Vietnam, Chinese migrants came to pay tribute especially because of his literatus status. The majority of the migrants came from Hokkien-speaking regions, while many also came from Cantonese speaking regions, especially Guangzhou. If Cai did not speak Cantonese, a form of Mandarin might have been used on those occasions.

Chinese settlers and sojourners were embedded in the local society, where Vietnamese was the koine language. As a traveler passing through, Cai did not learn the language himself, but he recorded Chinese migrants' different degrees of Vietnamese skills. Sim Liang from Zhao'an of Fujian, for example, was an official interpreter (*tongyan*) who helped Cai communicate with the Vietnamese officials at the beginning of his trip. While Sim successfully helped Cai navigate routine inquiries, he could not interpret the words from the head officials of Quảng Ngãi during a meeting. Cai noted that "the interpreter only knew the common street language, and not much more." Able to understand a more literary speech or not, Sim was kept outside the subsequent conversation.[70] Meanwhile, people like Trịnh Đức Hưng, Hồ Bảo Định, and Nguyễn Nhược Sơn came from Chinese migrant families and were well integrated into Vietnamese society and officialdom. While some of them could still speak the Quanzhou dialect of Hokkien, their mother tongue may have been Vietnamese.

Besides Vietnamese, literary Chinese was also used across different linguistic groups, but almost exclusively among the literati. Unlike the previously mentioned languages, it was purely a written form. Its spoken counterpart, Old Chinese, was spoken from around the sixth to the third century BCE, and the native speakers of it might have started to die out around the first century BCE.[71] However, its written form remained as the main communication form, perpetuated by the literati taste and by the civil service examinations since the sixth century CE.[72] By Cai's time, literary Chinese, together with the literati culture, was well established in Korea, Japan, and Vietnam. As a result, the literati of these countries could communicate by writing in literary Chinese, or as they called it, "brush talk" (Ch. *bitan*; V. *bút đàm*).[73] In addition to words and meanings, verification of each other's literati status was communicated in these conversations.[74]

Cai's trip testifies the use of literary Chinese in trans-linguistic communications. When he first arrived in Vietnam, the coast guard officials questioned him about the shipwreck through ink and brush. During his encounter with the head officials of Quảng Ngãi, the provincial administration commissioner Nguyễn Bạch and the surveillance commissioner Đặng Kim Giám, they also switched from Sim Liang's interpretation to brush conversation. Afterward, both the Administration Commission Office and Surveillance Commission Office followed up by sending him civil examination questions, requiring him to write literary Chinese essays by the morning of the next day. While Cai formulated this inquiry as Nguyễn and Đặng's appreciation of his literary talents, very likely it also served as a verification of Cai's self-proclaimed status as a government-sponsored student. Only then was Cai invited back by the commissioners and introduced to their staff members. Being honored as Mr. Stipendiary Student (Ông Lúm Sinh), he socialized with them through brush talks. In Cai's case, literary Chinese substituted for Vietnamese, ranging from bureaucratic to social communication.

In addition to literary Chinese, some Vietnamese wrote in the demotic script, chữ Nôm. Chữ Nôm, or as it is usually called, Nôm, formed characters in two ways. In the first, Chinese characters were used for their phonetic value, representing Vietnamese words that sounded similar. In the second, new characters were created that combined Chinese characters in novel ways, using one character for its phonetic value and another for its semantic value. This resulted in characters that adhered to the rules of Han character formation but were not in use in China.[75] During the Nguyễn dynasty, literary Chinese was favored for government documents, and Nôm was used mainly for poetry and literature, representing the sound of spoken Vietnamese. Cai Tinglan uses at least two Nôm words in his account, but likely merely copied them down without understanding the nature of the script. A reader of Chinese would not readily understand the principle of Nôm character formation.

Literary Chinese as the language of this *Miscellany of the South Seas* also conceals the multilingualism Cai encountered in Vietnam. For example, the place-names, personal names, and even proper names might have been uttered in Vietnamese, Hokkien, Mandarin, or Cantonese, but they were all conveyed in Chinese characters without phonetic specifications. Only occasionally would Cai record the differences between the Vietnamese and Chinese pronunciation of a place; but again, he used characters to signify these differences. And it is difficult to tell whether the characters were supposed to be read in Hokkien, some type of Mandarin, or some other language (table 1.1).

This poses a challenge to our translation: What romanization should we use to best convey these names? Our aim is to maintain both the multilingualism Cai encountered and the universalism of literary Chinese as the language of the travelogue. Since conventionally it is the mission of translations to go beyond the verbatim meaning of the target text, we used romanizations of different languages instead of just Modern Standard Mandarin pinyin to transliterate the characters of the proper names. For example, instead of rendering 沈亮 as Shen Liang, we rendered the name in Hokkien, as Sim Liang. We recorded Vietnamese place-names and personal names in the *quốc ngữ* script representing Vietnamese pronunciation, even though Cai was not a Vietnamese speaker. Writing in literary Chinese, Cai not only hoped his travelogue would be read by people in his circle in Qing China; he also recognized that the literati in Vietnam, and even in Korea and Japan, could read it.

Vietnamese Social History

Although the quotidian world of Vietnam was less important to Cai than recording the names and conversations he had with Fujian natives and Vietnamese officials, he provides an invaluable and rare glimpse of early Nguyễn social history. He can be a maddening guide; he recorded what he thought was significant but not necessarily what his modern readers would want to know. Women barely appear in this account. He recognized Chinese influence but was not always as observant of other strands of Vietnamese culture. He also makes mistakes. Some of the

TABLE 1. Cai's recording of place-names with different pronunciations

Characters	Pinyin	A reconstruction of nineteenth-century Mandarin	Hokkien pronunciation	Vietnamese
栗萬	lìwàn	lei?4 wan1	lit⁸ ban⁵	Lộ Vạn 潞潤
坐萬	zuòwàn	tsɔ3 wan1	tsɔ⁴ ban⁵	Chợ Vạn 幣潤
龍回	lónghuí	luŋ1 huei1	luŋ² hue²	Đồng Hới 洞海
坐輪	zuòlún	tsɔ3 lun1	tsɔ⁴ luən²	Chợ Luân 幣崙
據輪	jùlún	ky3 lun1	kuɪ⁵ luən²	Cố Luân 固崙

On five occasions, Cai used Chinese characters to denote the "Tang pronunciation" (*Tangyin* 唐音) of certain Vietnamese place-names. This chart records these five occasions. The "Tang pronunciation" characters are included in the first column from the left. Columns two, three, and four show pronunciations of the characters in modern Mandarin (denoted by pinyin), in nineteenth-century Mandarin based on *A Dictionary of the Chinese Language* (1815–1823) by Robert Morrison (denoted by International Phonetic Alphabet), and modern Hokkien dialects (denoted by International Phonetic Alphabet). The fifth column records the corresponding Vietnamese place-names in Chinese characters as Cai wrote them, together with the Vietnamese pronunciation. For the nineteenth-century Mandarin pronunciations in Morrison's *A Dictionary of the Chinese Language*, we follow the construction of Kaname, "19 shiji Hanyu guanhua yinxi yanjiu." For the Hokkien pronunciations, we follow Changji, *Minnan fangyan dacidian*.

names he records as officials of a particular place do not match Vietnamese historic records.[76] Nonetheless, he still created a valuable, though incomplete, portrait of daily life in Nguyễn Vietnam. Researchers can consult his work to learn more about social customs, agriculture and economics, and the functioning of government.

Cai Tinglan's account is unique as a lengthy eyewitness account of precolonial Vietnam written by a Qing subject. There are other accounts of Vietnam during this time period, notably European and American accounts. Alistair Lamb's anthology of British accounts of Vietnam, *The Mandarin Road to Old Hue*, provides an instructive comparison.[77] All foreign boats arriving in Vietnam had to be inspected and pay customs duty (in Hội An, 12 percent of the value of goods) upon arrival and departure and port fees that varied by country of origin. In addition, a gift to the official in charge of foreign trade was customary.[78] Euro-Americans tended to find these fees too high, opaque, and unfair. Cai Tinglan arrived in Vietnam by accident and sought only permission to return to China overland rather than wait for improved sailing conditions; in contrast, British and American visitors sought to secure favorable trading relations. Their demands ranged from privileged trading rights to ownership of islands to use as trade depots. Blocked at every turn from winning these unreasonable concessions, British and American observers concluded that the Nguyễn government was despotic, corrupt, or controlled by China. They may have misunderstood the trading system that used Chinese junks for long-haul ocean routes while Vietnamese merchants dominated riverine and coastal trade in the lower Mekong and Gulf of Siam. Europeans and Americans obsessed over gift-giving etiquette, imagining that there was a complex and corrupt gift-giving ritual that would unlock the country, if only they could figure out what kind of bribe was required. Assuming that larger gifts or bribes could ease their way, they became angry when that strategy failed. What European and American visitors failed to see was that the Vietnamese government rebuffed their demands because it was not in their self-interest to give in. Much English-language scholarship, like that of Alistair Lamb, has adopted these assumptions and has viewed the Euro-American failure to achieve their aims in a sympathetic light. In their disappointment and their misunderstanding of Vietnamese culture, Euro-American described the Vietnamese officials they encountered in patronizing ways, as "greedy" or even as "human baboons."[79]

Compared to these clumsy and unsuccessful overtures, Cai Tinglan was like a fish in water. Of course, he had an advantage in that he was not officially representing the Qing government or trying to wrest concessions from the Nguyễn. Unlike American and English sailors, he describes several warm and meaningful exchanges with Vietnamese scholars. He rarely used patronizing language to describe Vietnam or Vietnamese people, in contrast to some of the prefaces and postscripts of his text by other Chinese scholars. Preface writers like Zhou

Kai were not only dismissive of Vietnam but also characterized Cai's hometown as "poor and lonely," so perhaps Cai could sympathize with Vietnam's perceived marginality. Cai seems at ease, too, with gift-giving. He accepted some gifts (medicine) and declined others (money), without the obsessive strategizing typical of Anglo-American gift-giving in Vietnam. All that was required of him in exchange was poetry and calligraphy, and he was mostly happy to oblige. While the English perceived gift-giving as a kind of code of bribery that they could not crack, Cai used gift exchange to form affective relationships and get things done. Gifts were valued for their meaning, because people liked them, or as a memento.

During the Minh Mạng reign, a governor-general (a political appointee drawn from the military) oversaw two provinces. A provincial governor oversaw each province. Three officials operated at the next level down: the provincial administration commission, the surveillance commissioner, and what Cai Tinglan calls the garrison commander.[80] Taken together, Cai tells us, these three positions constitute the Office of the Three Officials. According to his report, Cai Tinglan met mainly with provincial governors and provincial administration commissioners. These were men with similar educational backgrounds to his own.

For Cai, Vietnam was familiar enough that exotic elements could be noteworthy. For example, Vietnamese officials dressed in a similar fashion to their Chinese counterparts, making the uniquely Vietnamese elements—namely "black crinkly silk embroidered headbands, black robes with narrow sleeves, and red damask trousers with bare feet"—all the more strange and remarkable.[81] Likewise, the social niceties and bureaucratic paperwork that were required for dealing with government were familiar to Cai, but he especially noted the *ta*, or platform daybed, and a copper tray for sharing gifts. He was at times exhausted by the attention he received as a foreign scholar, much in demand for calligraphy samples and poems.

He makes some note of military installations and architecture. Cai gives a very detailed description of the capital city, Huế, describing its battlements and cannons, designed with some European influence.

Although he was at times bothered by the incessant rain that soaked his clothes and bedding, he notes that "the scenery is quite similar to Taiwan." Bamboo, betel, and bananas were cultivated near villages, with rice fields nearby. Cai sees peacocks and pheasants, and he describes forests still teeming with apes. He noted that "tigers cause a lot of problems in the mountains" and gave a detailed description of how they were captured to aid in the training of war elephants.

Cai made some observations of religious life. While passing through the dangerous mountain roads to Hải Vân Pass, he noted twenty shrines to an efficacious deity called Bản Đầu Công, who protected them on the way. Later in the narrative, he noted that people worship Bản Đầu Công in their homes and that he is similar to the Tudi Gong, or Earth Lord, in Fujian. We can understand Bản Đầu Công as a generic local god.[82] Although Cai does not necessarily connect Bản Đầu Công with overseas Chinese, this name is connected with a deity that is worshipped in other diasporic Chinese communities of Southeast Asia. Historian Edgar Wickberg writes that "Pun Tao Kung" was an "exclusively Chinese deity . . . a kind of culture hero who was venerated by the Teochiu and Hakka Chinese of Thailand." In the Philippines, the topic of Wickberg's research, Pun Tao Kung is remembered as a crew member on the fifteenth-century Zheng He voyages who died and was buried there. In 1790, two Chinese merchants built his shrine. He was a patron of the Chinese community.[83] The deity's name appears in a temple in the Cù Lao Chàm islands and as a street name in Georgetown, Penang, and other Chinese communities across Southeast Asia.

Cai Tinglan visited both the shrine of the Trưng sisters, who led a rebellion against Han dynasty rule in 40 CE, and the shrine of Ma Yuan, the Han general who successfully put down their rebellion. Cai was taken to the shrine of the Trưng sisters in a village outside Hà Nội, which still stands and is now well within city limits. The Ma Yuan temples are near the Sino-Vietnamese border, and indeed, he was taken to one on both sides of the border. We can see Cai passing through different geographies; the Trưng sisters were deified in their home district, while Ma Yuan, a figure who knit together Vietnam and China, was important in the border zone. Coix seeds, or Job's tears, known for its ability to prevent miasmatic diseases and said to have been brought back to China from Vietnam by Ma Yuan, grew outside the Ma Yuan temple in Vietnam.

The dancing girls and entertainments Cai Tinglan enjoyed in the province of Lạng Sơn at Vietnam's northern border have been cited as an example of the economic robustness and integration of the upland border zone. The influence of Chinese migrants into the area from the mid-eighteenth century led to the formation of trading posts that provided lodging, food, and entertainment. The outlying northern provinces of Vietnam may have been more economically integrated with southern China than with the Red River delta.[84] Cai Tinglan's experience bears that out, although he traveled along the more sparsely populated tributary route and not on the commercial route nearer to mining sites to the west.[85]

In his third chapter, "Vietnam Chronicle," Cai Tinglan provides an overview of Vietnamese history. His understanding of early Vietnamese history is conventional and apparently drawn from Chinese texts, as he uses names for Vietnamese rulers prevalent in Chinese texts as opposed to in Vietnamese texts. His perspective on more recent history does not entirely conform to Vietnamese official history and probably reflects the understanding of his interlocutors, providing a valuable counterpoint.

A standard history would explain that Nguyễn Phúc Ánh, a scion of the Nguyễn royal family of southern Vietnam (Cochinchina), fled during the Tây Sơn uprising, gathered support abroad, and eventually prevailed against the Tây Sơn and established the Nguyễn dynasty in 1802, reigning as the Gia Long emperor. In Cai Tinglan's telling, Nguyễn Phúc Ánh was a sworn brother of the Tây Sơn founders who ruled his own kingdom in the south and moved against the Tây Sơn because of his anger over internal politics. While this is not entirely accurate, it may reflect the weary perspective of local residents. Rather than the imperial trappings of the official record, these rulers come across as members of a militarized brotherhood. Nguyễn Phúc Ánh was the sole survivor of a Tây Sơn massacre of Nguyễn royal family members in 1777. Building his power base in Saigon, Nguyễn Ánh solicited all the support he could—from Siam, France, and overseas Chinese communities. From 1778, Nguyễn Phúc Ánh controlled three southern provinces; he mobilized troops, collected taxes, appointed officials, redistributed land, and contacted foreign powers to seek recognition as a ruler.[86] This situation persisted for a relatively brief period, until 1781. He was at war with the Tây Sơn, not allied with them, but it is not surprising that residents of Đàng Trong may have described this period of multiple power centers to Cai Tinglan in a way that did not distinguish between the Nguyễn and the Tây Sơn brothers.

Likewise, Cai foregrounded Nguyễn Phúc Ánh's sponsorship of the Chinese pirate He Xianwen, adding a dimension to our understanding of the Tây Sơn-Nguyễn war. It is well known that the Tây Sơn employed Chinese pirates to aid their war effort. However, the case of He Xianwen has only recently been used to demonstrate that the Nguyễn, too, sponsored pirates. This is because the Vietnamese records memorialize them as heroes and admirals rather than as pirates.[87] Chinese emigrants (some of them pirates) contributed in various ways to both sides of the conflict.

Cai Tinglan repeats what he must have been told about Nguyễn Phúc Ánh's conquest of the Tây Sơn, his control of Hà Nội, and his accession to the throne as the Gia Long emperor. The Gia Long emperor's power base was Saigon, then known as Lũng Nại or Gia Định. Hà Nội, too, was historically known by several names, including Đông Kinh (Tonkin) and Thăng Long 昇龍 (Ascending Dragon). Cai writes of Gia Long:

> He changed the name of Lũng Nại to Gia Định [Auspiciously Settled 嘉定] and the name of Đông Kinh to Thăng Long [Ascending Prosperity 升隆]. He changed the reign name to Gia Long [Auspicious Prosperity 嘉隆], because he started in Gia Định and succeeded in Thăng Long.

Gia Long did indeed change the character for Long in Thăng Long from 龍 (Dragon) to 隆 (Prosperity), but this was not until 1805.[88] It is a common assumption that the Gia Long emperor chose his reign name to symbolize the unification of the north and south of his newly created empire by incorporating the characters of Vietnam's two major cities into his reign name. This assumption has been challenged based on the timing of the change of the *long* in Thăng Long several years after Gia Long adopted his reign name.[89] Even if the story is apocryphal, Cai Tinglan's account suggests that it dates to as early as 1835. On the other hand, given the highly symbolic nature of reign names, there is reason to think that Gia Long purposefully used meaningful names to promote national unity—even if the alteration of the characters for Thăng Long came second.

Cai Tinglan's Chinese perspective at times does not pair up with Vietnamese perspectives. For example, when Cai arrives in Lạng Sơn, the local magistrate informs him that Lạng Sơn and Cao Bằng are still recovering from the Nông Văn Vân rebellion (1833–35). Nông Văn Vân was an ethnically Tày native chieftain (*thổ ty*) and led local people and Chinese miners against the Nguyễn government. The fact that Chinese joined in the rebellion was not lost on Cai's Vietnamese interlocutors, who told him so. Cai objected, writing:

> Since this their king is more wary of Tang people, but they do not know that the chief instigators were all local people. There were only one or two foreigners among them who were cunning and took the opportunity to secretly attach themselves to them or were coerced into it against their will, but then as a result tens of thousands of migrants lost the favor and gained the enmity of the king, and even traders were subjected to higher taxes. Is it not unjust?[90]

Although not all of his observations can be taken at face value, Cai provides a trove of information that can deepen our understanding of Vietnamese society in the early nineteenth century.

NOTE ON TRANSLATION

We chose to render the names of people Cai Tinglan describes as Fujian natives in the Hokkien pronunciation. It is possible that these people had been living in Vietnam for a generation or more, so transliterating the names in the Vietnamese *quốc ngữ* script would have been an equally good choice. Likewise, we transliterate some names into Cantonese. When Cai describes something as "Tang pronunciation," we transcribe it into Modern Standard Mandarin. Pronunciation and transliteration systems are not stable, so our efforts almost certainly contain inaccuracies. Moreover, characters can be read and pronounced in any number of dialects and languages; there is no intrinsically standard, correct, or authentic way. Attentive readers may notice other inconsistencies. For example, we chose to render 海幢寺, a monastery in Guangzhou, in Cantonese pronunciation as Hoi Tong Monastery rather than the Mandarin pinyin Haiyinsi. This reflects the most common usage in English, our target language. For the same reason, we render 澎湖 as Penghu, not Phêⁿ-ô·, the Hokkien transliteration. Likewise, to maintain consistency with other secondary works, we designate the author in pinyin as Cai Tinglan. Careful readers may object to some of our choices, but we hope to provide a relatively seamless experience for general readers. Our aim in transliterating the characters of the original text into multiple languages is to highlight the diversity of the communities Cai Tinglan encountered and the multiple linguistic registers he moved through. This diversity is not as apparent in the original, written in Chinese characters, which can be pronounced multiple ways, or in the Vietnamese translation, which renders all names in Vietnamese pronunciation.

Take, for example, the title *Hainan zazhu*. The Chinese reprint gives no clue as to the meaning of this title, and the Vietnamese translation simply transliterates the sounds into Vietnamese. *Zazhu*, "miscellany," is uncontroversial, though it could be translated in other ways. Cai surely chose this word to reflect the different genres of his three chapters: shipwreck narrative, travelogue, and historical outline. But what did Cai Tinglan mean by Hainan? Hainan is the large island off the coast of Guangdong that was an important transshipment depot between Fujianese and Southeast Asian ports. But Cai did not travel there or even mention it in his account. The common phrase for coastal and maritime Southeast Asia inverted the term, Nanhai, or more commonly Nanyang, the Southern Seas. But Cai clearly chose Hainan intentionally and did not simply mistake it for the term Nanhai. Cai intended to cross the Taiwan Strait but ended up much farther south. This suggests that by *hai* he means the Taiwan Strait. Given his love of poetry and frequent forays into a literary register, we see that the title can be read as romantic and evocative, a "miscellany of the sea and the south." The first chapter deals with the sea; the final two chapters deal with the south. Nonetheless, we have chosen to render it instead as *Miscellany of the South Seas*, attempting to capture the general meaning.[91]

Translators make innumerable decisions, choosing between literal translation or more loosely conveying the sense. Cai Tinglan refers to all the officials he met by a formal title, though it is not always clear if he is always using their real titles or employing titles of his own devising. We chose to render these titles in English to promote readability. We have used Charles O. Hucker's *Dictionary of Official Titles in Imperial China* when we could, consulted Đỗ Văn Ninh's *Từ Điển Chức Quan Việt Nam* (Dictionary of Vietnamese official titles), and made our own translations for more unusual titles. In some cases, such as *prefect*, we translated more than one title the same way to avoid unwieldy phrases like "prefect of a superior prefecture." The original terms can be found in the glossary. Cai Tinglan uses *gong* as a salutation for officials and *jun* for degree holders or teachers who do not hold official positions. We translate them both as "Mr." Interestingly, Cai Tinglan uses "Vietnam" throughout his text, not the Chinese name "Annan" or the Vietnamese name Đại Nam, "Great South" (officially adopted only in 1839). He uses "China" (Zhongguo) to designate his own country, but he also uses "Tang" to designate Chinese people or pronunciation.

Some terms deserve special attention. Cai Tinglan uses the character 庯 to designate trading settlements dominated by overseas Chinese. Following Li Tana's suggestion, we transliterate this word as *phố* and translate it as "market town."[92] Vũ Đường Luân refers to *phố* in the northwest frontier zone as "trading posts," noting that these border trading nodes were not extensive enough to justify being called "town."[93] Based on the appearance of the term in the 1806 imperially commissioned gazetteer of Vietnam, *Hoàng Việt Nhất Thống Dư Địa Chí*, *phố*, or market towns, were closely associated with populations of Chinese traders and served in part as transshipment depots for sending products from mines and other forest products abroad.[94] Cai Tinglan mentions three *phố*: Quảng Ngãi market town, located thirty *li* outside of Quảng Ngãi city; Hội An market town, located twenty *li* outside of Hội An; and Khâu Lư, in Lạng Sơn near the Chinese border. All three are clearly dominated by Chinese traders and led by Chinese headmen. Khâu Lư is more of a border trading post, and Cai explicitly notes that traders from Guangdong and Guangxi are allowed there. The distance from other towns is not surprising; at this time, the Chinese trading center Chợ Lớn (literally, "Big Market") was some distance from Bến Nghé.[95] It was only later that the city of Saigon, now renamed Hồ Chí Minh City, grew to absorb both areas.

It is also noteworthy that Cai Tinglan refers to the southern country as "Vietnam" throughout the text. As mentioned above, Vietnam was first adopted as the official name of the country at the beginning of the Nguyễn dynasty as a compromise. Initially, the Gia Long emperor had proposed Nam Việt (Ch. Nanyue). This name was rejected by the Qing court because it evoked the rebellious Han-era kingdom of the same name. Despite the compromise, Qing sources continued to refer to Vietnam as Annan ("the Pacified South"), while later Vietnamese sources tended to prefer Đại Nam.[96] Cai Tinglan's use of "Vietnam" suggests either that the term was more widely used than scholars have assumed or that Cai was trying to use the most correct and official name of the country. Indeed, when the American war sloop *Peacock*, sent by President Andrew Jackson, arrived in Vietnam just a couple of years before Cai, the Vietnamese would not accept the letter from President Jackson because Vietnam was mislabeled as "Annam" and the emperor was mislabeled as "king."[97]

Cai Tinglan frequently provided definitions and made asides. To mark out the secondary nature of these comments, as was common practice, they were carved in script half the size of the main text. To preserve this sense, we have set the subscripts in italic font and enclosed them in parentheses. When we insert our own definitions, dates, or updated names, we use square brackets. We have organized the index alphabetically using pinyin for ease of use and to follow scholarly convention.

Cai Tinglan may have felt that he was treading the world's wild edges during the fearful days adrift at sea, but once he landed on solid ground, he found fellowship. He indeed gained a fuller view of the world from his interactions with Nguyễn officials and Fujianese merchants, giving his work a tone of sympathetic understanding that sets it apart from other contemporary works on Vietnam by foreigners. For us, one of the most enduring aspects of *Miscellany of the South Seas* is the importance of conversations and friendships that cross linguistic and national boundaries.

MISCELLANY
of the SOUTH SEAS

By "Source of Fragrance" Cai Tinglan of Penghu

ZHOU'S FOREWORD

Mr. Cai Tinglan is a scholar from Penghu. In the spring of *renchen*, the twelfth year of the Daoguang reign [1832], I took up my post to aid Penghu through the Xingquan Yong Circuit [in Fujian], and he came to visit me with a poem tucked in his sleeve and told me that the people were suffering from famine on account of a storm. I wrote a poem to respond to his. He asked to be my student, and because his name was Lan [Orchid], I gave him the style name of Xiangzu [Source of Fragrance]. I instructed him on our predecessors' methods of studying.

Penghu is one of the islands in the sea in Taiwan Prefecture; the soil is alkaline and unsuitable for growing wheat or rice. Yams, taro, and some other grains grow there. The people are accustomed to fishing, and the sea provides their livelihood. There are no schools, but they are allotted four licentiates under the prefectural school. Because there were no books on the island for him to read, he went to the county and studied hard; he tested at the highest level and became a [government] "stipendiary student." When he would cross the sea for the county level examination and stay in Xiamen, I would often test him at Jade Screen Academy.

In autumn of the *yiwei* year (*the fifteenth year of the Daoguang reign*) [1835], while returning from the examination he met with a hurricane and disappeared. In the summer of the following *bingshen* year (*the sixteenth year of the Daoguang reign*) [1836], he returned from Vietnam and described his hardships in detail. Moreover, he brought to me Vietnamese envoys' regards (*in the summer of the* renchen *year [1832], the director of the Ministry of Works, Trần Văn Trung; the vice director of the Ministry of Rites, Cao Hữu Dực; and the envoy Trần Văn Tuân escorted Li Zhenqing, formerly of Zhanghua county [in Taiwan], and his family to*

Xiamen. In the winter they returned to their country. We sent them off with poems). I celebrated his rebirth and paid for his expenses to return to Penghu.

That autumn, after I was transferred to Taiwan, he compiled "Record of Danger on the High Seas," "Travelogue of the Fiery Wastelands," and "Record of Vietnam" for me to review. I read his text and marveled. First he writes of how in the midst of a storm upon the dark sea, being battered by billowing waves and hanging between life and death, he remained calm inside, thinking only of his old mother. Then he writes of Vietnam's obedience to the Qing, their high estimation of the Heavenly Empire's literati, and how he matched poetry with the literati there. He even discusses the real state of its historical mountains, rivers, roads, passes, city walls, palaces, granaries, treasuries, and markets. Next he narrates Vietnamese history, sketching the past but detailing the present thoroughly and completely, and examines their customs accordingly. Ah! You can call his journey extraordinary. I was worried that growing up in his poor and lonely island hometown, even if he studied hard, he would not be able to have many novel experiences. Did not heaven intend to open his thoughts and senses to improve his writing through this experience?

The Grand Historian [Sima Qian] said, "I have traveled west to Kongtong, north to Zhuolu, east to the ocean, and south to the Huai River." That is why his writing was erudite, provocative, and extraordinary; no later writer has been able to reach his level. When scholars travel, they should always contemplate the local mountains, rivers, people and related affairs. Everything that can provide a broader perspective and reference points is called learning. And since he traveled to a faraway land, of course he had something worth writing about. Besides, Vietnam is Nanyue, where in the past, Lu Jia went, gathered a lot of gold, and came back. [In contrast], he [Cai Tinglan] was lost and empty-handed, but he was prudent in what he declined and what he accepted—how can we compare him to Lu Jia? Now he has selected tribute for the court. If he will use this as his calling card, to show to the important people, there must be ones who can reward him.

Su Ziyou [Su Zhe] said, "When it comes to mountains, I have seen the height of Mount Song and Mount Hua. When it comes to rivers, I have seen the width of the Yellow River and the Yangzi River. Gazing upon palaces, I have seen the grandness of the world."[1] If he had traveled there, it could not compare in retrospect to his travels in Vietnam. The benefit to his writing is boundless.

~~~~~~

Composed by Zhou Kaizhong of Fuyang county [Zhejiang]

LIU'S FOREWORD

When [Su] Dongpo lived in Dan'er, he wrote this poem: "I would not regret dying nine deaths in the southern wastes / Traveling to exotic places is the crowning glory of my whole life."[1] That is why among his exceptional writings, the masterpieces are the ones about foreign places. Dan'er is part of Qiongzhou [Hainan Island] in Guangdong, across the ocean.[2] In the Song, it first became part of the Southern Tang; however, the gentry who stop their oars there now would not consider it exotic.

Without treading the world's wild edges, one cannot gain a full view of the world. Mr. Cai Tinglan of Penghu whetted his moral integrity and enriched his literary ability. At both the annual examination and the imperial examination, he was always the champion of his class. Unfortunately, although he was repeatedly recommended, it never worked out. After the autumn examination in the *yiwei* year of the Daoguang reign [1835], he sailed from Xiamen and suddenly encountered a storm. He drifted through ten dark and stormy nights and arrived in Vietnam. The king of Vietnam gave him resources to return overland, and he only returned the following year in the summer. When I read in his "Record of Danger on the High Seas" about the hurricane whipping between the islands, the churning tides, the waves as high as mountains, the boat's mast snapping and the rudder bending, the way the boat sank and then bobbed back up, and about how he cried out to the spirits on his hands and knees, begging for his life, I sighed and wondered how heaven could endanger him like that. Afterward, I read in his "Travelogue to the Fiery Wastelands" that the king highly regarded Confucian teachings; their civil and military officials of high and low rank all said, "We were not expecting to meet a scholar from the Heavenly Court today!" Wherever he went, there was never a day without a feast. Once tipsy, they always requested poems from him, and those who could responded in verse, alternating rhymes. When it was time to part, they clasped his hand and wept, saying, "From the northern to the southern ends of the world, times of parting are easy to find but times of meeting are difficult to come by." I could not help but sigh and yet felt happy, saying that although heaven had threatened his life, the people of distant lands loved him to this extent. When I finished reading his "Record of Vietnam," [I learned that] Vietnam, in the past called Yuechang, was through the Qin, Han, Tang, Song, Yuan, and Ming sometimes united with China and sometimes divided, sometimes in order and sometimes chaotic, and about the changes in districts, counties, and prefectures, the depths of the mountains, rivers, and valleys, the characteristics of the flora and fauna, the different customs for rites and music and caps and gowns, and about their unique customs. He meticulously wrote about [these topics] that are not recorded in the biographies of foreigners in the Twenty-seven Histories, but he still called it a "brief chronicle." I could not help feeling happy and surprised, astonished and appreciative. He indeed managed well the heaven-sent danger and well deserved the people's affection. Now his record will take its place with Dongpo's overseas essays and narratives. Truly, he traveled to "exotic places" without the regret of "nine deaths."

With that said, I have even more with which to recommend him. When one's state of mind is fixed, then one can endure extreme circumstances; when one's experience is broad, then one can investigate the situation of all things. If one has confidence and a calm heart, then even in the face of disaster after disaster, one will come out unharmed. A respectful and faithful scholar can walk among the barbarians. Admittedly, if not for the fact that his whole life he has been recommended but has not achieved his due, wouldn't we still say his character is like that of Dongpo's from beginning to end? Now I can see it from his travels. This is my foreword.

On the sixteenth day of the first month of autumn, the sixteenth year of Daoguang reign (1836), which is the year of bingshen, Liu Hong'ao [1778–1849], a friend from the Surveillance Commission of Shaanxi and the Military Defense Circuit of Taiwan and Penghu, style name Cibai, wrote this.

FIRST DEDICATION

~~~~~~

Jiang Yi'an ([style name] Yong)
Mr. Sima

~~~~~~

The essays had not yet been received for the triennial exam, when the ship was buffeted by wind and waves and nearly flew away.

He drifted between sky and water for ten days and nights, through smoke and clouds he could dimly discern that the wind was changing. (*They abandoned the mast and were then pushed by a northwest wind / luckily it turned into a northeast wind, and they were able to reach Annam. Otherwise they would have directly entered the current* [luoji].)[1]

To the south, they would have encountered the perils of uninhabited islands and huge waves; to the north, they could see that they had lost the peaks of home.

Back and forth, navigating ten thousand miles of sea, he came back with a sack of poems.

On his journey home, he passed through Guilin, he arrived safely at Heron Gate [Xiamen], and I was fortunate to hear news of him.

His mother, waiting anxiously for him at the gate, was consoled.

Those who cherish talent would be convinced by their evaluation: (*Circuit Intendant Zhou [Yungao] of Xiamen and Liu Lianfang of Taiwan both regard him highly and were looking forward to seeing him*).

Reflecting on the frightening mist-covered waters, only now settled, his attachment to his homeland was deepened.

Powerful wind and waves drove him far away, and he strolled through danger, assuming an important mission.

SECOND DEDICATION

~~~~~~

Xu Yinping ([style name] Deshu),
Scholar of Broad Learning

~~~~~~

The raging waves drenched his worn-out clothes,
Even through nine deaths he would not forget to care for his parent.
His heart like a furled flower, his body like the leaves,
Preserved by heaven to proclaim parental love.
At Thới Cần estuary he was interrogated and submitted the copper tray,
A lone sojourner sailing ten thousand miles.
The elders of old Yuechang were extremely pleased;
diligent students came to visit the Han-clothed gentleman.
Su [Dongpo] spoke softly within the winding peaks, entreating the
    bound Hundred Yue to return.
Gathering the herb of heaven and earth to fill his sleeves, how many
    people pass the Ghost Gate in their lives?
He readily wielded the brush, matching verses, like Xiangshan's [Bai
    Juyi] fame that reached Rooster Forest [Silla].[1]
And now he [Cai Tinglan] does not write of banalities [as with Bai Juyi's
    poems]; one piece of new poetry is worth a piece of gold.

MISCELLANY OF THE SOUTH SEAS

RECORD OF PERIL ON THE HIGH SEAS

At the end of the fall of the *yiwei* year of the Daoguang reign [1835], I finished the metropolitan examination and was on my way home to the south. When I arrived at Xiamen (*also called Heron Island*), it was the time for the birthday of my teacher, circuit intendant Zhou Yungao. (*At that time he was the intendant of the Xing[hua]-Quan[zhou]-Yong[chun] Circuit, stationed at Xiamen.*) I followed the group in raising a glass, happily feasting for several days. Then I crossed over to Jinmen (*Jinmen isle east of Xiamen*) to go to my ancestral home (*where my family has lived for generations*). At Liaoluo (*Liaoluo station on the southeast side of Jinmen*), I found a boat. I was on my way back to Penghu to pay my respects to my mother (*who at that time had moved to Penghu*), and then I planned to go to Taiwan, thinking that I would arrive in less than ten days. (*That year I was lecturing at the Yinxin Academy in the prefectural seat of Taiwan.*)

On the second day of the tenth month [November 21, 1835], the sailors came to urge me to go. I led my younger brother Tingyang along with some attendants to hurry to the seaside, where we saw that the boat had already pulled up the anchor (*which was made out of heavy wood; oceangoing vessels use them to stop the ship*), hoisted the tall *phâng* (*the main sail; the common [Hokkien] name for "sail"*), and was about to leave. We hurriedly hailed a small boat and pumped the oars until we caught up. As the sun sank in the west, we saw strands of clouds floating over the sea to the southeast, mixing continually with dark blue mist. This lasted a long time before dissipating. When night fell, the whole sky was full of bright, twinkling stars. I pointed out that this is a sign for upcoming wind and advised the sailors that we ought to slow down our advance to the sea (*the unbounded part of the ocean is what I call "sea"—*

there is the inner sea and outer sea). The captain insisted otherwise. We saw that a few boats near us were also gradually losing the coast. I was already seasick, so I flung myself into the cabin and curled up under the quilt, holding my breath, listening to where we were going. After three watches, I heard the wind whistling and the keel of the boat slapping the waves.[1] It made a sound like boulders crashing, powerfully jolting the boat. Although I could barely withstand it, I still reasoned that the winds and waves of the open water could certainly be that strong, so for the time I disregarded it. Again we burned watch incense and waited (*on the boat, we used a stick of incense to measure the watch, and we called it "watch incense"*). After the boat sailed fast for more than two watches, I thought that we had already passed over the Black Ditch (*in the sea there is the Blackwater Ocean, where the water is deep and black, and the easterly current is fast and shallow, called "the Black Ditch"*), and that we would come ashore in the morning. The boat sailed on faster, the waves were even higher, and the wind was raging.

At first, the sailors said that black clouds were massing in the northwest. The clouds sped to the southeast, galloping like horses. A fierce wind arose in a flash, the seawater was churning, and the boat listed to the side as though it would flip. I was in the cabin, reeling from side to side. It was hard to remain seated or lying down. As I shook with fear, I heard the sailors shouting, "If we go east, we are going to crash against the coast! Quick, turn the rudder to go back!" The wind was so violent, the rudder was dragged under the water and the *hàkim* [下金] got jammed (*the hàkim is located in the back of the boat under the water; it is used to fasten the rudder*). More than ten people pushed it without budging it. Then they lowered the sail and jettisoned their cargo, hoping that if they lightened it, the boat would go. When the day dawned, everywhere we looked was hazy. There were white breakers as tall as mountains, with our solitary boat bobbing on the waves. The compass still indicated southeast, but we did not know which ocean we were in. We went on like this for three days. The sailors said, "If we're lucky, this will take us to Siam or Luzon, and we will still be able to go back. But if we crash into Nan'aoqi [Nan'ao Island off the northern coast of Guangdong], then we will *luoji*. (Luoji *means "entering the current." The water is especially deep, and once you enter it you cannot get out. From Nan'aoqi you would be blown into the One Thousand Li Stone Embankment and Ten Thousand Li Sandy Shoal, which are just south of the Taiwan Sea.*) Then our lives are over."[2] The prevailing wind seemed to be somewhat calmer. We all gathered around a small fire to eat and had our fill.

After a short while, the Mazu flag started to flutter (*the Empress of Heaven, we commonly call her Mazu*).[3] The wind was now coming from the northeast, whistling and howling, raging and surging. Droplets of water seemed to be everywhere. We were soaked through as if in a downpour, wet from head to toe, cold inside and out. We stared at one another, our faces drained of color. Suddenly, there was the sound of enormous waves. The front of the boat shook as though we had crashed against stones near the shore. The boat sank into the water but immediately started to rise again. The *sêngkài* and wooden boards around the cabin all started to float (*the walls and ceiling of the cabin are called "sêngkài"*) as the water deluged the cabins and flowed out the other side. I was submerged and fell prostrate, sure I would die, but my brother grabbed a rope and, sobbing, tied it around my waist, heaving it up to the deck while falling to his knees to entreat heaven to spare our lives. The sailors were all wailing in grief. I called out to the *chhut-hái* (*the captain is called "chhut-hái" or "the one who goes out to the sea"*) saying, "Crying is no use! Quick, chop down the main mast!" The mast sank into the water and the boat started to calm, drifting along with the waves as light as a duck.

Because we saw that the water in the water tank was almost gone, it was sealed up and we were forbidden to draw water. We cooked taro with salt water to make our morning and evening meals. I fretted, thinking the water would not get us through. The next day I ate a little piece of taro and surprisingly forgot my hunger and thirst.

After four or five days, we saw a white bird soaring in the air. The ocean had turned a faint black color, and then a faint blue color. We expected that mountains were not far off. As the sun was about to go down, we saw a faint line among ominous dark clouds in the distance.

It seemed to be stuck to the water and motionless, taking on the shape of mountains. When the morning broke and the mist evaporated, the array completely unfolded in front of our eyes. A few *li* away from the boat, I saw three small islets towering above us.[4] They were covered in lush green vegetation and trees, surrounded by upright boulders, all forming a peril [for our ship]. Our ship floated with the tide, wending whither it went. We recognized that the approaching sails were all *kahpán (the name for foreign boats)*, going back and forth continuously like shuttles on a loom. Seeing that those mountain ports had arrayed masts, like a big harbor, we all went wild with excitement, falling to our knees and thanking heaven.

In the afternoon, it drizzled in bursts, clouds gathered, the wind and rain arose. Miasmic mist obscured the view in every direction, the mountains blurred into the mist, and the facing sides were obscured from one another. The current gained speed, and billowing waves rose to the sky, striking the ship fore and aft. The shaking sounded like thunder, buffeting the ship until dusk. At around the first watch, we all thought we had run aground, and we all made our own plans. I asked myself if my life would end now. Clutching my brother, we sat and awaited our fate. Not long after, the wind stopped and the rain ceased, and even the waves settled down. We leaned out of the cabin and saw the moon in the east. Through the blackness we suddenly saw rays of sunlight. Peering into the distance, I sensed that we were encircled by mighty peaks to the north and south, as though we were approaching the coast. We cast in the "lead clock" to test it (*the "lead clock," made of lead, is a device with a rope knotted every ten feet to measure the depth of the water*). The water was twenty or thirty feet deep. Beneath us was fine sand. We lowered the anchor and settled in. Counting on my fingers, I guessed it was the eleventh day of the tenth [lunar] month [November 30, 1835].

At daybreak, we saw a fishing boat passing by and conversed with it, but we did not understand their language. They wrote the two characters 安南 "Annam" with their fingers. After a while, a small boat came over, with a person who could speak Chinese [*huayu*] in it, who called

himself a "Tang person" (*Annamese call Chinese people "Tang people"*).[5]
When I boarded the boat, he was stunned and asked, "You are from
China? How did you end up here without knowing the port route?"
We all told him what happened. He shook his head and was speechless.
He said, "If spirits had not been watching over you, how could it be
like this? The first islets you approached were the Chiêm Tất La islets
[Chàm islands], with a strong current flowing on their east and west.[6]
In the center is a very narrow port, and ships cannot get in unless they
go with the tide because they sink as soon as they hit boulders. Going
west and then south from there, one can reach the inner harbor. But
you had no mast or sail, so you could not reach it against the current.
Its east and west sides are known to be extremely dangerous. The ocean
floor is covered by reefs and a shoal (*stones on the ocean floor are called
"reefs," and sand is called "shoal"*), which are dozens of *li* long. The way to
the harbor is circuitous. Even old fisherfolk do not know it well. Make
one mistake and you would have been broken to bits." I heard this and
felt even more afraid.

I remembered my Penghu home in the middle of the ocean. Since
childhood I played in the vast ocean, and I have crossed it dozens of
times, all times peacefully and without fear. Wind and waves are to be
expected, but nothing like the present dangers that we experienced.
The chance of surviving was one in a million. I have heard that the
ancients relied on loyalty and sincerity to cross rough seas, treading
through peril as though it were solid ground. Through dangerous conditions, they [sat at ease], sheathing their swords and resting their jade
ornaments, talking and laughing normally, all without changing expression. Those were sages and heroes with honest minds; their thoughts
all resonated with heaven. Therefore, heaven could not bear to take
their lives from this world. I asked myself how someone as insignificant
as me, with no qualities to speak of, although I do conduct myself with
loyalty and sincerity, could be jolted into these dire straits. How could
I not be terrified? My heart was pounding, playing through scenes of
my old mother. My final thoughts were of unfiliality. How could I still
dare to think of the life ahead? I could only put my fate in the hands of

heaven. Now I am surprised that I am alive and that I have arrived at this place. I did not realize that heaven would treat me so generously, that even though I washed up empty-handed in a distant wasteland, poverty stricken and depressed, I could still use poetry to earn a name in a foreign country.[7] Who could have predicted that? But it is a fortunate thing. We all had our breakfasts, eating our fill without restraint. Then we sat around basking in the sun. Our wet clothes dried out, but the tracks of our tears had not yet faded away. I hastily recorded it.

Master Zhou Yungao's commentary: [Cai Tinglan] wrote about facing danger, fully describing the bizarreness of the situation and his shock. At the end of this section, he wrote his innermost feelings, allowing us to see what kind of person he is.

TRAVELOGUE OF THE FIERY WASTELAND

~~~~~~

By "Source of Fragrance" Cai Tinglan of Penghu

~~~~~~

Our boat was moored within Vietnam's borders. The next day, which was the thirteenth day of the tenth month of the *yiwei* year [December 2, 1835], two coast guard officials rode a boat alongside our ship. They both wore black crinkly silk embroidered headbands, black robes with narrow sleeves, and red damask trousers with bare feet. (*Vietnamese officials go barefoot inside and out. They do not differentiate between summer and winter clothes. In the winter they still wear lightweight clothes. The high ranking ones tend to use blue and black for headbands and robes, but they all wear red trousers.*)[1] They brought along one interpreter (*the one who communicates is called the interpreter*) who spoke Hokkien (*he was from Zhao'an County [Fujian] and his name was Sim Liang*). He addressed the captain and said, "These are the guard officials of the Thới Cần station in the Tư Nghĩa prefecture of Quảng Ngãi Province (*one was called Nguyễn Văn Loan, one was called Nguyễn Văn Lợi*).[2] They had heard that a Chinese ship had been blown off course and arrived here, and specially came to inspect it." We invited them to board our ship, checking the cabins and all around the ship. Before they left, they asked how we ended up here and took our license (*in their country they all use Chinese characters, and the documents they use in the yamen are similar in form to those in China*). They implored us to move the ship into the inner harbor the next day and to follow the custom of submission to superiors with a copper tray. (*Each time they give people gifts, they always put them on a copper tray and enter kneeling while handing the tray overhead. This is called the submission of the copper tray.*)

On the second day near midday, we saw dozens of bulrush sails flying toward us; they were all fishing boats. The interpreter preceded several people boarding the boat: some grabbed the rudder, others pulled up the anchor. They fastened a rope from each of their small ships to our ship's bow, then the small ships plied their oars and dragged us in. Our ship slowly started to move. A mariner's song rose in the air, and they all sang it together, a call and response echoing across the water.[3] Soaring overhead, the gulls flew off when they heard the people's voices resounding through the air. At dusk we entered a river. We saw nearby mountains and verdant bamboo forests with impenetrable foliage. Smoke from cooking fires was rising from several hamlets. We soon reached the bank. There were more than ten thatched buildings, and the guard station was there. The guard officials personally came out to the beach to direct the fishing boats and ordered them to moor in front of the office. Once our ship was anchored, the fishing vessels left. (*It is an old rule of their country that when ships enter the station area, the guard officials do all they can to protect it in front of the station office. They bang a gong in front of the government office, and fishing boats gather like ants to run errands, and they do not dare to demand pay.*) In the middle of the night, the garrison drums sounded *dum dum dum* until dawn. (*The night watchman's drum sounds all night. They hit the drum once for each hour instead of according to the number of the hour. The high officials then ring a bell.*)

On the fifteenth day, we accompanied the interpreter to the shore. The captain brought along the goods from the ship (*ginger, flour, tobacco, tea—all the things people in that country like*). We presented them as gifts on the copper plate; I also added writing brushes and ink. The guard officials were pleased and invited me to sit on the platform. (*Officials high and low do not use tables and chairs. They often set up a short platform in the center. The most respected sit in the southern direction, and they set up platforms to the left and right, facing the east and west. The hosts are on the left and the guests on the right, as in the Han system. The esteemed sit at the inner side, and the junior sit at the outer side accordingly.*) They quickly prepared a letter to rush off to report to the provincial governor. (*High officials stationed at the province are called provincial governor, and those in the prefecture are called prefectural governor.*)[4] We thus borrowed a *fang* of rice (*approximately four* dou) and one string of cash. (*These were lead coins stamped with the Minh Mạng reign date. Two could be exchanged for one copper coin. Each string had six hundred.*) Then we took our leave from the guard officials and returned to the boat.

On the afternoon of the sixteenth day, we saw that two "wheels" had been lifted on the bank (*sedan chairs are called "wheels"*). A person sat in each of the "wheels," and behind him were several people, holding rattan whips. After a short time, the same guard officials boarded our boat. Then they called out to the interpreter, "We are sent by the provincial governor to verify the case." (*One was Trần Hưng Trí, who was an unranked functionary of the provincial administration commissioner, and the other was Nguyễn Tiến Thống, who was an unranked functionary of the surveillance commissioner.*) According to our license and the number and names of the travelers (*they called recorded passengers on oceangoing vessels "travelers"*), they ordered that we each extend the middle finger of our left hands and stamped it, calling it "finger marking." They again carefully examined the cabin to make sure that there were no forbidden goods. (*Opium and weapons were the most strictly forbidden. If found, people would be convicted as pirates and sentenced to decapitation.*) Then they measured the ship's dimensions, the cabin's depth, and compiled a register in order to levy taxes. (*If the ship had no merchandise, then we would pay no tax.*) They took out brush and ink, and each wrote on their papers, asking and answering questions. They arranged for me to meet with the high officials in the province, and then left.

The next morning, they really did board a small boat and invited us [to join them], and I went with the captain. There was a gentle breeze and the water was calm; we floated downstream for more than ten *li* and then came to the bank. When the sun was at its height, we followed small footpaths between field edges for about two or three *li* until we came to Lộ Vạn market.[5] (*In Tang pronunciation, it sounds like Liwan. It has a garrison of soldiers.*) That night we stayed at the interpreter's house. The next day, we rose at the fifth watch [3 a.m.] and walked in the light of the moon. We could hear the night watchmen's rattles sounding from village to village. Deep in the alleys, the barking of dogs sounded like panthers, and frogs croaked ceaselessly in the ponds. After we had gone a bit more than twenty *li*, the sky brightened, and we had our meal beside the road at a simple stand. Then we again went for more than a *li* and crossed a stream. The two functionaries competed in asking me to sit in their sedan chair, but I declined. Therefore, they called the soldiers to usher me at a strolling pace. (*The officials had no bailiffs, so they rely on soldiers to provide services.*) The main road was more than two *zhang* [6.4 meters] wide (*there is only one highway in their country, going directly north-south*), and jackfruit trees were planted on both sides. There was one tree every ten paces. Their leaves and branches intertwined, and the ground was completely in the shade. A light breeze was blowing, and I felt the coolness through my collar and sleeves. In the distance we saw a vast area covered by level farmland, planted with glossy rice paddy. People cultivated bamboo all around their houses with many banana and betel plants; the scenery was quite similar to Taiwan. There were bridges across the road all made out of layer upon layer of old and new bamboo poles. They were raised up on horizontal beams. It felt supple when I stepped on it. In the afternoon we crossed another river. More than a *li* away from the river, we were approaching Quảng Ngãi Province, which had one provincial administration commissioner, one surveillance commissioner, and one garrison commander stationed there. (*The position "fan" they call provincial administration commissioner and "nie" they call surveillance commissioner.*[6] *The commander they call Ông garrison commander. The three positions together they call the Office of the Three Officials.*) There was a small city (*locally called Cù Mông*), which had gates at the east, west, and north with a government office, a warehouse, and a military barracks inside the city, and most of the residents and market outside the city.[7] (*In every provincial capital, the people did not reside inside.*) When we went to the market, we encountered a Tang person (*in that country they call Chinese people Tang people, or they call them "people of the Heavenly Court." They can be easily recognized because of their shaved hair*), Lim Sun (*he was from Tong'an [in Fujian]*), and he invited us to his home.

A short time later, the functionaries met with the high officials. I wore formal clothes to enter the city, and gawkers laughed at me.[8] When I arrived at the office, I was led into a large hall. (*The government office had only one large room, where morning and night all affairs took place. The staff members all gather in the hall to handle the cases. Afterward they leave the hall and go home.*) Two officials were sitting in the middle. The interpreter murmured to me, "One of them is the provincial administration commissioner, Mr. Nguyễn (*Bạch*), from the royal house, and the other is the surveillance commissioner, Mr. Đặng (*Kim Giám*)." Therefore I bowed to the front. They both rose, took a good look at me, and laughed heartily. The whole room was surprised.[9] They pointed to a platform on the left and asked me to sit. They murmured something to the interpreter, and the interpreter could not pass it on to me. (*The interpreter knew only the common street language and not much more.*) The officials themselves wrote on a paper, asking my native place, my profession, and how I came to be blown here. I wrote back in detail the whole of our story. They nodded and sighed, seeming deeply sympathetic. They summoned the head of the Fujian Association Teng Kim (*from Tong'an*) to choose a building to settle me down in.[10] (*The Tang people were mainly from two places, Min [Fujian] and Yue [Guangdong]. The Min are called the "Fujian Association" and the Yue are called the "Guangdong Association." Each association has a headman to organize affairs.*) First they distributed to me two *fang* of rice and two strings of cash for daily use. Then they called the ship captain to enter, allowing him to give permission to open the cabin and to sell the remaining goods. I rose to thank them, then quickly retreated to stay at Lim Sun's house.

On the nineteenth day, I wrote a missive and asked the association headmen to send it [to the officials]. [After receiving it,] the high officials praised it, so they prepared a document and attached our missive to be delivered to the king. (*The king lived in Phú Xuân city [Huế], a seven- day journey from Quảng Ngãi Province.*)[11] That night, the provincial administration commissioner ordered the clerk to bring us a piece of paper with examination questions on it (*one on the Four Books, one on classics, and another on shi poetry and fu poetry*), with a deadline of the next morning at seven before they would come to get it.[12] The next night, Mr. Đặng also sent the scribe with examination questions (*with the same number of questions as in the case of the provincial administration commissioner*). I answered them all within the allotted time and left them for their inspection. They kept the answers and did not return them to me.

On the twenty-second day, I took my leave and returned to the boat.

On the twenty-fourth day, my brother and I took all our luggage, bade farewell to the sailors, and returned to Quảng Ngãi Province. We never went back to the boat after that.

~~~~~~

On the twenty-sixth day, the high official heard that I had arrived; he ordered every staffer (*one provincial magistrate, two local magistrates, two registrars, two county magistrates, one county deputy, and one instructor*) to come out and meet me. Because the residence was narrow, they just greeted me and then left. I did not have a chance to learn their names. The next morning, I went to wait for the high officials. Everyone was present; therefore, I thanked them for meeting with me. Then there happened to be a big meeting for a criminal interrogation, so I just left. Several days passed, during which an unending stream of officials and gentlemen made every excuse to come visit me. They called me "Ông stipendiary student" (*they locally call respected people* ông, *or they call them* thầy [*teacher*]), and they asked for a sample of my writing.[13] I could barely put up with their interruptions. Only the provincial administration commissioners Bùi Hữu Trực and Nguyễn Sĩ Long and I had friendly and sincere relations.

On the fifth day of the eleventh month, the high official received the king's decree, so I hurried to the office. They read out loud a copy of the vermilion comments that said, "The above-mentioned was born to a literary household. He unluckily met with a storm and exhausted all of his travel money. It is truly pitiable. Already that province has given him money and rice. In addition, we would like to demonstrate our kindness by increasing the gift by fifty strings [of cash] and twenty *fang* of rice, enabling him to have money for his expenses, to demonstrate our solicitude for this unfortunate scholar from the Heavenly Court. And give each of his shipmates one *fang* of rice every month." I then wrote a letter to express my gratitude and went to the storehouse to receive provisions, of which there was no lack. From this point on, the high officials increased their respectful treatment, and in their leisure time, they always came by to engage in brush talks.

On the ninth day, a new palace graduate named Mr. Lê (*Triều Quý*), accompanied by the provincial magistrate, Mr. Phạm (*Hoa Trình*), came to visit me. Mr. Phạm had formerly served as an assistant envoy and had presented tribute to the Heavenly Court [of the Qing]. He had written a collection of poetry and pulled it from his sleeve to show me. I meticulously commented and praised it. Then I also wrote a poem for him as a present.

On the tenth day, I met Ng Bun (*from Longxi county [Fujian], currently living in Quảng Ngãi market town*). He said that he had returned to Fujian three times overland. (*There are two routes to return to Fujian. The one from Qiongzhou in Guangdong passing Chikan in Hainan is the outer route, but there are robbers, so you must go in a group. The other one is the inner route through Guangxi; it is comparatively far, but you do not have to worry about being ambushed by bandits.*) He said he was very familiar with the situation of the route. I was very pleased and then decided to go home. The next day I sent a letter to the high officials and asked for a loan of travel expenses so that I could take the overland route back home. Because it was against precedent, the high officials were reluctant. (*The precedent: for every Chinese boat that was blown off course and arrived here, if there are civil or military officials or members of the gentry or scholars on board, they are always accompanied by a government boat to bring them back to China. Merchants are the ones who return overland.*) I strenuously entreated them, so they sent a missive to the king to request permission.

On the thirteenth day, I went to Quảng Ngãi market town (*places* with merchants are called phố, or "market town." *Quảng Ngãi market is thirty li from the city, and Chinese boats gather there*) and stayed at Ng Bun's house. I had a great time talking to him about our hometowns. The host also asked his wife and kids to greet me. The Tang people all rushed to visit me. I stayed at Ng Bun's for two nights.

On the twentieth day, a private tutor named Trần Hưng Đạo used a poem to invite me for a drink. I looked at what books the children were reciting: the Four Books, classics, history, ancient literature, poetry; they were all the same as in China. And they were all handwritten manuscripts. Some people used bamboo pens to write on bricks that were smeared with mud.[14] The [learning conditions] were very poor. (*Writing brushes and ink were in short supply, and there were no writing books to follow in writing characters.*) The others held paper on their palms and write in cursive script, really quickly. Mr. Trần truly understood the classics and history, and he also knew poetry. People called him "Ông Teacher." (*Teachers are called* thầy.) From then on, more and more people invited me to drink.

On the sixth day of the twelfth month, the king sent the envoy Bùi Kính Thúc (*he was a Provincial Graduate and about to become a county magistrate*) to visit. He personally came to my residence and very warmly consoled me. The next day he came to thank the high officials, and they all gathered in the provincial hall. The envoy and high officials surmised the king's intentions and all urged me to abandon the land route and go by sea. They agreed that the next spring, when the winds from the south start up, they would prepare a government ship to escort me to Xiamen. All present thought that that would be most convenient. Citing my haste to get home to my mother as my reason, we wrote back and forth from 7 a.m. to 1 p.m. My request became more and more insistent, and the envoy started to change his mind. He agreed that when he reported to the king, he would ask the court to decide. Then he immediately returned that night. I was homesick and anxious, which was turning into a full-blown illness, and I could not get out of bed for ten days. The high officials sent people to comfort and ask after me from time to time.

On the nineteenth day at daybreak, the man who had previously inspected our ship, Mr. Trần Hưng Trí, came in to congratulate me: "The office has granted permission!" I leapt up as though my illness had immediately dissipated and asked him about it. Master Trần urged me to straighten my clothes and go before the high officials. The high officials showed me the reply of the office and a copy of the king's vermilion comment, which said, "Since the person repeatedly requested to go home overland, it is difficult to keep him for a long time. It is more reasonable to assent to his request. The Ministry of Revenue will grant ten *liang* of silver for the travel expense. The officials of the province should arrange his trip well." When I finished reading it, I wept and thanked them. I spoke with the high officials about setting a date for my departure. As his tears fell, Mr. Đặng said, "While it is very good that you are returning, hereafter we will be poles apart, north and south. When will we ever meet again?" Nor could I overcome my sadness. I went back and ordered my brother to purchase what we needed for the journey, borrowing servants as travel companions, and then I went to bid farewell to my acquaintances.

The next day, the high officials sent over the money from the Ministry of Revenue and my traveling papers (*they delegated a representative, in charge of twenty soldiers, to escort me to Quảng Nam. They also gave me other travel papers to exchange for fresh soldiers along the way, and support for rations*), as well as an extra fifty *liang* of silver. Mr. Đặng also sent a retainer on his own with cinnamon and an ivory container [for writing brushes]. I took all of them and expressed my thanks with poems. The scribe Bùi Hữu Trực also made me a gift of three strings of cash, and the fellow townsmen Lim Khiám (*a Tong'an person*), Lim Sun, Teng Kim, and that group gifted me with medicines. I declined money from others who offered it.

⌇⌇⌇⌇⌇⌇⌇⌇⌇⌇⌇⌇⌇⌇⌇⌇⌇⌇⌇⌇⌇⌇⌇⌇⌇⌇⌇⌇⌇⌇⌇⌇

At daybreak on the twenty-first day, I went to bid farewell to the high officials and left a thank- you note, asking them to give it to the king. The high officials walked me from the office. From the provincial magistrate on down, they prepared a farewell ceremony outside the city. Several people from the town gathered to see us off beside a creek, and tears fell as we parted. The ship captain and the passengers all stayed behind, waiting until a ship could come and escort them home. I calculated that I had resided in Quảng Ngãi for more than fifty days, during which time it had mainly been overcast and rainy with impenetrable mist. The ground was so muddy that one could barely take a step. Clothing, shoes, beds, mats were always damp, and mosquitos and flies circled night and day. On the rare occasions when the sky happened to clear, I had to socialize with the high officials and others without a break; nor did they have any gardens in which to while away the time. Therefore I paced around in boredom, and I felt stifled and uncomfortable. Now that it was suddenly time to start on my homeward journey, my brother and I were like cranes sprung from a cage, shaking our wings toward the firmament without pondering the ten thousand miles left to travel.

From Quảng Ngãi city we traveled forty *li* to Lộ Vạn, one *gong*. (*Each* gong *is forty* li; *each has a barracks set up*.) It was windy and rainy the whole evening, so we spent the night at our interpreter Sim Liang's house. On the second day, we traveled forty *li* to Khân Bản. (*From Khân Bản we could board a river boat and reach Quảng Nam after one day and night of travel*.) Twenty *li* past the river, we arrived at Vạn market (*in Tang pronunciation it is called Zuowan*).[15] In another one hundred and sixty *li*, we reached the Quảng Nam provincial capital (*commonly called Hội An; its provincial city was called Tọa Quì*). We lodged at the place of the headman of the market town, Hồng Tèng (*from Tong'an in Fujian*). Twenty *li* from the city was the market town Hội An (*where Chinese people were most numerous*), there was an old transport commission depot which was really spacious. (*Inside they offer sacrifice to every commissioner from the previous dynasty, but Chinese people do not maintain the sacrifice well. Now it has returned to local people's protection. It is often blocked off, and people are not allowed to go in*.)

On the twenty-fifth day, I saw the provincial governor (*he was also in charge of Quảng Ngãi [in addition to Quảng Nam], so he was called Nam Ngãi provincial governor*), Mr. Phan.[16] (*His name was Thanh Giản, his literary name was Plum River, he was a palace graduate, and once went to the Heavenly Court as an envoy.*[17] *Previously he had served as the grand secretary of East Hall, because of some accident he was demoted to provincial positions, and was moved to the current post.*) He was full of erudition, modest by nature, and down to earth about rites and protocol. He invited me to chat twice on the same day and gifted me five strings of cash and several cakes of tea. We wrote poems responding to each other. The next morning, he sent a staffer with his name card to see me off.

On the twenty-sixth day, we went on the Quảng Nam road. I saw that the seedlings were really lush, and the new sprouts were like a beautiful mattress of green. Egrets stood motionless in the field, and trees were hazy in the distance. The Three Tower Mountains in the ocean stood distinctly, facing down one another. (*There are three rocky mountains in the ocean that are called Three Towers.*[18] *There is a large cave opening, making a natural house. The popular saying was that there were seven spiders nesting in it. They turned into beautiful women. Later they were destroyed by the Buddha. Now it is called the Seven Sisters Cave.*) Rising approximately two feet from the ground [*sic*], they look steep.[19] That night we lodged at a station at a mountain's foot. The *wangfu* (wangfu *means sedan-bearer*) admonished me to get up early the next morning to eat well and then climb Narrow Pass. (*This mountain range was the highest and steepest along the way. It is one of Vietnam's most difficult passes.*)

When the sun was just starting to rise, we left the hostel and traveled about two *li*. We were in the mist the entire way. When I raised my eyes to the ridge, the clouds were piled like a snowbank, fading off into the sky, so I could not see the peak. When the morning sun had already risen, we passed one small mountain ridge. The winding path bore up along the seacoast, and we could hear the waves crashing and the larger waves roaring, echoing across the rocks and valley. We reached the entrance to a small village; there was a coast guard official guarding it and he interrogated us very sternly. We skirted the edge of the mountains and then climbed a switchback plank road for more than ten *li*. Brambles and weeds proliferated along each side amid a bristling bamboo forest. There were

> birds warbling among the trees,
> a hundred kinds of bird call.
> Wildflowers were all in bloom,
> the ground covered with petals.

The scenery was indescribable. When we were halfway up the mountain, high up amid rocky peaks, there were fish-scale stone steps, like a thousand-foot ladder to the clouds. The sedan bearers held the sedan chair horizontally on their shoulders and proceeded, and our guards all came to their aid; lifting their knees and straining their chests, the sweat dripped off their backs like rain. After seven or eight *li*, we approached the summit. We rested beneath an old tree. Looking up, we saw a solid rock wall against which hung a board made of redbud wood that was a few *chi* thick.[20] It said, "Ocean Mountain Pass" [now Hải Vân Pass]; there was a guard and dozens of elite soldiers stationed there.[21] It was ringed by weapons and cannons; truly a flying bird could not cross it. I climbed the pass and looked down. To the north was the vast endless ocean with masts coming in and out of view like so many gulls drifting across blue green. In front of the peak there were ports to the east and west; the interior was crisscrossed with streams that could hold a thousand ships. The clear water was pleated by waves, with even lines of whitecaps, and sun and shade playing across the surface of the water was enough to clear one's heart of all cares. To the southwest was a deep bamboo jungle, home to a herd of elephants. Deer and apes proliferate within it as well, making this wilderness unfit for human beings.[22] The largest among old-growth trees on the mountain were several hundreds of *wei* around, with intertwined branches, making a thick canopy overhead.[23] Apes and monkeys scrambled around in packs, jumping up and down when they saw us. (*In the mountains there are many apes that go around with linked arms; the local people call them the "ape generals."*) Soon, the wind howled and whistled across the tree-tops, making a desolate scene. I quietly descended. Bidding farewell to the guards, we left the pass and traveled six or seven *li*. Day turned to dusk, and we lodged for the night in a rustic person's home. It was freezing that night, so I burned scraps of wood by the bedside to warm myself and my younger brother.

The next day we got a late start. We went two or three *li* through dense forest and came out to the right of the peak. When I looked

FIG. 1. "The scenery was indescribable." Photo taken in the general area where Cai Tinglan made this observation. Photograph by Kathlene Baldanza.

FIG. 2. Hải Vân Pass. Photograph by Kathlene Baldanza.

down from the top, we saw that it was jutting out over a precipice that was so deep I could not see the bottom. Then I got out of my sedan chair and asked two men to assist me in walking. Backing against the stone cliff, I stepped on the concave part of the steps. After three hundred steps, we rested under a stone ridge. Resuming our forward progress, we passed three small peaks that were all jagged and steep. After about ten *li*, we started to reach level ground along the coast. We followed the coast for several *li* until we arrived at a large stream. After crossing the stream, we came to a small town to the north with a station where we were inspected. The sedan bearers said to me, "When we climbed the peak and came here, we passed more than twenty shrines. (*[The deity in it is] locally called Bản Đầu Công; he is very efficacious.*) Passersby continually toss incense and paper. It is due to his protection that though people go through this area every day, they are untroubled by snakes and tigers." The pass was opened in the reign of Gia Long. (*Gia Long was the reign name of the current king's father.*) It is right in the center of Vietnam; if one person guards the pass, even ten thousand people would not be able to besiege it. Therefore it is called the Narrow Pass. It is 140 *li* to Phú Xuân [Huế] (*and it is a hundred* li *away from Quảng Nam in the south*).

On the thirtieth day, we went to Phú Xuân city [Huế] (*popularly called Thuận Hóa city*). The city wall is constructed in brick and is very sturdy and well built; it is more than a *zhang* [3.2 meters] high, spanning four or five *li*, and has eight gates, with small, narrow towers. Every hundred steps there were five huge cannons linked together on top of the wall, all covered by pavilions, looking like a flock of birds with outstretched wings. The outside of the wall was surrounded by a moat. (*The water is deep, and it does not dry up.*) Beyond the moat there is a stream.[24] (*The stream is very deep and wide; it is connected to many streams inland, and it flows outward to the sea.*) Each warship and other kinds of ships big and small are lined up along the banks of the stream, covered by thatched canopies. Near the wall on all sides, the markets were bustling, with merchandise abundantly displayed, packed with people, and houses neatly lined the road.[25] When I reached the city, it was almost noon. The company commander (*company commander is the name of an official post; his job is like that of a leader of a thousand*) led us into the city to see the prefect of Thừa Thiên Prefecture, Mr. Nguyễn (*Thạc Phủ*), the vice prefect Mr. Lê (*Tiểu Hạ, with the title of palace graduate*). Mr. Nguyễn met me and then soon left. Mr. Lê was very eloquent. We wrote poems to each other, getting so immersed in writing out our commentaries that we lost ourselves completely. When the sun was about to set, I took my leave and went to New Market (*on a stream bank north of the city*) and slept at the house of Tân Chhin (*from Jinjiang county [Fujian]*). That day was the eve of Lunar New Year. Everyone was changing the couplets in their doorways and lighting firecrackers, just like the old traditions of seeing out the old year and welcoming the new in China. At such a sentimental season, I missed my family. My brother and I wept all night and did not sleep a wink.

The following year was *bingshen* [the thirty-third in the sexagenary cycle], the sixteenth year of the Daoguang reign [1836], first day of the first month (*in Vietnam it was the seventeenth year of the Minh Mạng reign*).

Approaching the celebratory start,
the celestial omens indicate the beginning of the year.
On the streets, in the city,
the foreign dancing and barbaric singing
and happy cries shake the ground.

I wrote a congratulatory essay and went with Hồng Liâng (*a person from Xiamen*) to the prefectural governor to extend my New Year's greeting and hoped that it would be sent to the king.[26] The grand secretary of the East Hall, Mr. Quan (*Nhân Phủ*), and the director of the

FIG. 3. Huế City walls. Photograph by Kathlene Baldanza.

Ministry of Revenue, Mr. Nguyễn (*Nhược Thủy*), happened to be at the prefect's office. My congratulatory essay was read and met with praise.[27] Mr. Quan wrote to instruct me, "Our country has a rule: when you hear the rooster crow at dawn on New Year's Day, all civilian and military officials come to the palace to send their New Year's greetings. They are given gold and sent out, and then the palace gate is sealed. They wait for the order to come down to open the gate, and only then are they permitted to come and go. Now if you wish to follow the proper ceremony of our country, I can wait until the door is opened, and then we send you for a visit. I think that if our king offers a boat to urge you to stay, you should not refuse. Otherwise, since you had received the previous order, you can go unimpeded with the paperwork from the provincial officials. Wait for seven days until they open the granary, and then you can receive provisions and set out. You can leave your congratulatory essay at the prefectural hall, and then I can personally convey the sincerity of your greetings." I had already decided to leave [soon], so I left and walked around the city center. The palace was located in the southeast corner facing Seal Mountain. (*The mountain is shaped like a scholar's seal. It is outside the city walls. On the mountain there are altars to the spirits of the mountains, rivers, earth, and grain.*)[28] Its appearance was magnificent; the buildings and pavilions at the top were a feat of engineering.

A golden calabash was placed on the ridge of the palace, and it was dazzling. The Meridian Gate was in front of the palace, and there was a huge flagpole on the road in front of it.[29] Battalions were arrayed on the left and right of the palace. The guards stationed there were drawn from elite troops and were well armed. A bit to the north lay the headquarters of the Generals of the Left and Right, where they had sixteen rooms to store the cannons and ammunition. The palace was encircled by a high wall with batteries in all four corners with redcoat cannons.[30] A deep moat had been dug all around the walls, more than a *zhang* [3.2 meter] wide. There were two layers of railings outside of the moat to keep out passersby who were not allowed in. They also built the Minh Viễn building in addition to the main living hall. Its upper windows were brightly lit with all the rooms shining brilliantly; it was used as

FIG. 4. Golden calabash adorning building in Huế imperial city. Photograph by Kathlene Baldanza.

a place for entertaining. There were several palaces to the west of the royal palace where the princes and their families lived. Farther west were the yamen of the inner high officials. Nearby to the northeast was the granary, which contained enough rice and provisions to last dozens of years. The rest was made up of civil and military government offices, barracks, palaces for royal relatives, and ancestral halls. There were few residents there.

On the second day, we went to a banquet with the officials of the Imperial Household Department. There was a crowd who had heard that I was a Chinese scholar and came to look at me one after another. The room was nearly full and I could not distinguish between the noble and the humble.

On the seventh day, I wrote a poem to say goodbye to the grand secretary of the East Hall and the officials of the Imperial Household Department. I hired a riverboat to take me to Nghênh Hạ (*place-name*). Mr. Lê personally escorted me out of the city. He ordered that several

FIG. 5. Cannons in Huế. Photograph by Kathlene Baldanza.

members of my escort go first by the land route and wait at Quảng Trị Province. Tân Chhin's whole family escorted me to the riverbank. I traveled by river for two days through fog and mist. Mountains on all sides turned day into dusk. The rain lashed against the sail and shutters; rivulets babbled through the reeds. The water had suddenly risen two or three *chi*.

On the tenth day at dawn, we reached Quảng Trị. (*From Phú Xuân to here is 120* li *by the water route.*) We moored the boat at a bend in the river and followed the boatmen ashore. We walked two or three *li* to the provincial capital. The soldiers had arrived earlier and were standing by the city gate. It was about to rain, so we hurried after a clerk to meet the provincial governor. (*He also served as the governor of Quảng Bình Province, so he was called provincial governor of Trị Bình*), Mr. Hà (*Đăng Khoa*). When he was lounging around half-dressed and scratching himself, he saw that guests had arrived; he straightened his clothes and angrily had the clerk whipped twenty times. I wrote to him,

"When we appeared he did not treat us rudely. Why is he suddenly being humiliated?" His countenance cleared and he rose to apologize, saying, "He did not notify me in advance. He made me panic, and I could not act appropriately. I was rude just now, but please forgive me." Then he invited me to take inspiration from our surroundings and match verses with him. He enjoyed my poems and invited me to spend the night, but I could not. I urged him to process my travel papers. He provided fresh men for our escort and sent some of them to Nghênh Hạ first to wait for us. I took my leave, and the boatman carried me on his back to the boat in the rain. We came ashore the next afternoon (*it is forty* li *by the water route from Quảng Trị to here*) and spent the night in Nghênh Hạ (*Nghênh Hạ is 240* li *from Quảng Bình*) and hired sedan chair bearers to set out again the next morning.

On the thirteenth day, we arrived at the provincial capital of Quảng Bình Province (*popularly called Đồng Hới; in Tang pronunciation it is called Longhui*), and we stopped at the market headman Hồng Kín's home (*he is from Tong'an in Fujian*). When I entered I saw the provincial administration commissioner, Mr. Ngô. (*His name was Dương Hạo, his style was Tông Mạnh, and his literary name was Cối Giang; he had been student at the Imperial College.*)[31] His expression changed as he rose and said, "Your clothing is not like that of common people. I hope that you will instruct me in verse." He called for wine and started to improvise poems. He really got into a lyrical mood, feasting all his followers with food and drink. When I was about to leave, he presented me with a handful of chicks and said he hoped I could come back the next day to chat more. The next morning he sent the clerk to hasten me. When I stepped through the doorway, he and the surveillance commissioner, Mr. Nguyễn (*Đăng Uẩn*), were just hearing legal cases. I hesitated and stopped walking. Mr. Ngô ordered the criminal to retreat and invited me to have a seat on the platform daybed. Again we exchanged poems with one another. He closely questioned me about Chinese customs, education, and people. After we had been sitting for a long time, lunch was brought in. We talked back and forth, paying most attention to state affairs. I felt moved [by our conversation] and lingered, not leaving until dusk.

On the fifteenth day, Mr. Nguyễn had business to attend to; Mr. Ngô personally came to the market headman's house bearing wine. Holding a cup, he said, "Today is the Lantern Festival, so we ought to sing and dance together to laud the magnificent night sky." He pulled out the cup and set it up for the wine. I declined and did not dare to stay. He saw the sedan bearers outside in the street and said, "How could I treat you so poorly?" He gave them three strings of cash as a gift as well as rows of couplets. I also followed his rhyme and composed a poem of thanks. He rushed out and hurried to the courier station near the gate. He set out a farewell meal on the mat and waited for us to arrive. He again served me three cups to see me off. With tears

FIG. 6. Imperial College in Huế (Quốc tử giám).
Photograph by Kathlene Baldanza.

streaming down, he held my hand as we passed through the gate [of Quảng Bình] and walked with me for about two *li*. Then he returned and climbed to the top of the gate, watching for a while, saluting me from a distance. Hồng Kín and Ngô Sim, both from the same county (*Tong'an*), brought their wives and children, each carrying medicine as a parting gift. They accompanied me beyond the gates for five *li* and bid me a tearful goodbye. Soon after, an escort of soldiers and officials arrived to accompany us. One of them had been a close attendant of Mr. Ngô, personally sent by him, and he served me on the road (*later, when I reached Hà Tĩnh, I sent Mr. Ngô poetry to thank him*). That night we stayed in Chợ Luân.[32] (*In Tang pronunciation it is called Zuolun, it is forty* li *from Quảng Bình.*) It was overcast, and the moon was obscured. The owner of the guesthouse had lit the lights and gathered a banquet to celebrate the Lantern Festival. I felt even gloomier.

From Chợ Luân we walked for two days to Chợ Ròn (*80* li *on the route*), through ceaseless driving rain. My clothes clung to my body; [the cold] penetrated my flesh, it was unbearably cold. From Chợ Ròn we crossed to the inner bank more than a *li* from the Ròn River and spent the night at Cồ Luân (*in Tang pronunciation it is called Julun*).

On the nineteenth day at daybreak, we walked twenty *li* to Transverse Mountain Ridge.[33] (*In Tang pronunciation it is called Buzhengling.*) We walked on a narrow steep road winding up the ridge for two or three *li*. A sign was hung across the summit inscribed, "Transverse Mountain Pass." There were guards defending it and dozens of pass soldiers guarding and checking [the pass] all the time as a major hub of the road to the north. After we crossed the pass, the mountains began to slope down, then the path started to straighten out for several *li*. We went for more than fifty more *li* and spent the night in Trung Cố (*place-name*).

On the afternoon of the twentieth day, we passed through Hà Hoa prefecture.[34] (*The prefectural capital was more than two* li *east of the road.*) After another three *li* we arrived at the provincial capital of Hà Tĩnh. We spent the night at the home of Wong Cat (*a person from Chaozhou in Guangdong*). The provincial administration commissioner Mr. Cao (*named Hữu Dực. In the* renchen *year of the Daoguang reign [1832], he had followed his king's command to escort the former county magistrate of Zhanghua [county in Taiwan], Li Zhenqing, and his family by boat to Xiamen. After returning, he was rewarded with the title Grand Master for Excellent Counsel*) was under the weather and did not come out to meet us. He sent a subordinate with a note to our residence to apologize, mentioning that he had been to China.

On the twenty-first day, Mr. Cao directed the local magistrate and the registrar to see me off. I left a note to bid him farewell and set off.

On the twenty-second day, I arrived at the provincial capital of Nghệ An (*it is 200* li *from Trung Cố to here*) and spent the night at Lim Sàn's house (*a person from Zhao'an [Fujian]*).[35] The four hundred *li* between Quảng Bình and Nghệ An was marshy. Our feet frequently sank in the muck, and it was hard to walk without slipping. Between the fields and wilderness, we would frequently travel dozens of *li* before we saw signs of human habitation. Travelers had to be prepared for bandits lurking in the wilds. The guest houses used *gu* poison to harm people. If they hide it inside beef and you eat it, then there would be no saving you. The antidote is foreign ginger.[36] (*Also called chili pepper, the seeds are from Holland, the flower is white and the stigma is green, when the fruit is cooked it turns bright red. It is filled with spicy seeds.*[37] *One can eat it with the hull. Some are long and pointed, some are round and slightly pointed.*) People add them to their food to guard against poison.

On the twenty-third day, we met the governor-general (*he simultaneously oversees Hà Tĩnh; he is called governor-general of Nghệ Tĩnh*), Mr. Nguyễn (*the governors-general are all related to the king. Mr. Nguyễn has so much prestige and power that people do not dare say his name*).[38] The clerk Trịnh Đức Hưng (*his family was from Dehua county in Fujian; he could speak the Quanzhou dialect*) translated for us. First he ordered four strong soldiers, swords dangling from their belts, to stand along either side of the hall. (*Ordinarily, when high officials ascend the hall, they do not line up according to insignia or call out the groups. Coming and going they do not make announcements in order to clear the road [for officials].*) We then were ushered in, exchanged a few words with Mr. Nguyễn, and then left. The two main officials, the provincial administration commissioner and surveillance commissioner, were on an official trip [so they were out of town]. There was the teacher Trần Hải Đình, the cultivated talent Hồ Bảo Định (*his ancestors were from Shunde County in Guangdong*), who came to compose poetry together. Mr. Hồ's poems were precise and fine; he had agility with words. From dusk on we lit one candle after another, only stopping when the rooster crowed.

On the twenty-fourth day, the escort came and asked about the departure date, and then we set out. The fellow-provincials from Fujian and Guangdong collectively gave three strings of cash, and they all accompanied us past the town. It drizzled for the ten *li* outside of Nghệ An, but luckily it was not so bad. There were many peacocks perching in the trees along the sides of the road, dazzling the eye with emerald green.[39] Their feathers were damp with rain, and the heaviness prevented them from flying far. When we were about to reach Thanh Hóa, there were many rocky mountains rising steeply a thousand fathoms high, towering and lofty, as though fashioned by spirits, carved by nature with magnificence beyond words. Peacocks and white pheasants were gathered in the heights. Cinnamon is grown in the mountains; it has a strong flavor that is better than that of Đông Kinh.

On the twenty-sixth day, we arrived at the provincial capital of Thanh Hóa (*240 li away from Nghệ An*) and spent the night at Sím Jim's house (*from Zhao'an County [Fujian]*).

The next day, we saw the governor-general, Mr. Nguyễn. (*There are many people with the surname Nguyễn in Thanh Hóa. Because these noble families are too hard to manage, the king uses his close relatives to govern them.*) He pointed to the front of the hall and requested me to write couplets to hang on the pillars. He was very pleased and called his sons out to meet with us. (*His eldest son could play the zither; he served as deputy guard.*) He wrote a letter admonishing garrison commanders on the road ahead to keep a watch at night. Then we met the provincial administration commissioner, Mr. Nguyễn (*his name was Nhược Sơn; his ancestors were from Fuzhou in Fujian. His uncle, now deceased, had been the minister of personnel*), and we received assistance from him. He offered one *liang* of silver and some good tea as a gift. He also sent word to Hà Nội, enjoining the Chaozhou and Guangdong interpreters and the market headmen to assist us with ten [*liang*] of silver. I was moved by his solicitousness and wrote a poem for him in return.

On the twenty-eighth day, instructor Ông Ích Khiêm invited us to his office.[40] Once we entered the door, he clasped his hands when he came out to greet me. We talked and laughed together. Making fun of himself for his low salary, he gifted me two strings of cash. Several of our compatriots came and collectively gave us three strings of cash; I thanked them all and returned it. As the sun was already high in the sky, I bid farewell to the high officials and set out on the road.

On the twenty-ninth day, we reached the provincial capital of Ninh Bình (*colloquially called Bình Sáng*) and stayed at the home of Zog Lam (*from Chaozhou in Guangdong*). Ninh Bình is 160 *li* from Thanh Hóa, covered by jagged mountains poking out sharply in bizarre shapes, and dotted with unfathomably deep caves and ravines. Flying Phoenix Mountain looms over the provincial capital, and within the city there is a smaller mountain in the front, like a screen. The two mountains used to be known as a famous scenic spot, because the imposing peaks grant travelers a good view. People have previously inscribed many poems on them.

On the first day of the second month, we met with the provincial governor, Mr. Nguyễn (*Ninh Bình also has a lot of people surnamed Nguyễn, so the king also uses his relative as the provincial governor to manage them*). He happened to be returning from reviewing the troops. I stayed for breakfast, and he called for his subordinate officials to keep me company and to play a poetry drinking game for fun. Just before I left, I was given a stalk of areca palm and five strings of cash. I took the areca and returned the cash. That day I traveled sixty *li* and spent the night at Lý Nhân Prefecture.[41]

On the second day, the provincial magistrate [*zhifuguan*] (*the "zhifu" is called "zhifuguan," and also called the "futangguan" or provincial governor*), Mr. Lê (*Tĩnh Uyên*), summoned me to drink.[42] I drained half a bottle and then left. (*They used a gourd as a wine bottle.*)

On the fifth day, I spent the night at Thường Tín (*it is 240 li from Lý Nhân*).[43]

On the sixth day, I called upon the provincial magistrate but did not meet him. As we passed Thường Tín and headed north, the land was fertile, and the local people were prosperous. The buildings became more gorgeous. After sixty *li* we arrived at the provincial capital, Hà Nội (*its ancient name is Đông Kinh, and it used to be called Thăng Long, but now it has been changed to Hà Nội*), stopping at the Fujian native-place lodge. We spent the night, then moved to the house of Cheng Thiam, fellow-provincial (*from Jinmen in Tong'an*).

On the eighth day, we met the governor-general, Mr. Nguyễn. When I sent in my card, he came out clasping hands and said, "I did not expect that today I would meet a scholar from the Heavenly Court!" Then we sat and had an intimate and moving conversation that lasted all morning, and only then would he allow me to go. Then I met the provincial administration commissioner, Mr. Trần. (*His name was Văn Trung. In the* renchen *year of the Daoguang reign [1832] he had followed his king's command to go to Xiamen by boat with Cao Hữu Dực. After returning, he was rewarded with the title Grand Master of Excellent Counsel.*) At the front of the hall was a brilliantly displayed table. He straightened his clothes and shoes and came out to meet us. He humbly and politely served me tea with his own hands. He inquired about things in Fuzhou and Xiamen as well as the officials and gentry that he knew there. He urged me to stay a few days, but I could not. He also gifted me ten silver taels, and I had to insist on rejecting it.

On the ninth day, the literati Can Jyu Sam, Can Fai Gwong, and Wong Bik Gwong (*they were all from Guangzhou in Guangdong, and were good at composing poems*) came to visit.[44] They said that Đông Kinh was large and rich in resources, its cities are strong, its markets bustling, it is the most affluent part of Vietnam, home to many scholar-officials and historical sites, not to be missed. They invited me into the city to see the palace of the Lê clan; the painted beams and engraved rafters as well as tall buildings with rows of attics are distinct amid greenery and mist. We passed the shopping district, where money was amassing

FIG. 7. Hai Bà Trưng Temple, Hanoi. Photograph by Kathlene Baldanza.

like clouds as I had never seen. We crossed the Nhị Hà River (*which used to be called Phú Lương River*) and checked out the hostel for envoys from the Heavenly Court (*on the left back on the Nhị Hà River*).[45] There were enormous stelae and stone tablets, creating an atmosphere of grandeur. We also went to Đồng Nhân Village to see the Temple to the Two Sisters. (*During the reign of Guangwu of the Eastern Han, the two sisters Trưng Trắc and Trưng Nhị rebelled. Ma Yuan came to pacify them. The two sisters died at Nguyệt Đức River. Their corpses floated back down the Phú Lương River, and the local people built a shrine to them.*)[46] We returned and spent the night at Jyu Sam's residence. Falling into a mood of nostalgia, we composed poetry back and forth all night. The more I reflected on past events, the deeper my feelings grew.

The next day I arose late. The Guangdong market headman, Ho Ji Hing, the interpreters Can Zan Gei (*both from Guangdong*) and Tîn Hêng Khoah (*from Chaozhou*) came with various people from the native-place lodge and gifted us with ten *liang* of silver accompanied with other things. The Fujian market headman, Sím Lim (*from Zhao'an*), came with various people from the native-place lodge and gifted us with fifty strings of cash. I gratefully declined and only accepted the medicine offered by Yeoh Ban Kì, Chia Kì (*from Changtai county [Fujian]*), and Hô Êng (*the former market headman, from Zhangzhou [Fujian]*), and Cheng Thiam and others. That day, the native-place lodges each set up farewell banquets. I thanked them all in poetry.

On the eleventh day, when I took my leave from the high officials Mr. Nguyễn and Mr. Trần, they decided to follow the precedent of seeing off high officials and dispatched fifty soldiers to escort us. I thought that this would be too costly and asked to retain the original number. In the afternoon we arrived at Từ Sơn Prefecture, but the provincial magistrate had gone out for some other business. At sunset we arrived at the provincial capital of Bắc Ninh Province (*it is 130 li from Hà Nội*).

On the twelfth day, we met the provincial governor, Mr. Nguyễn (*a close relative of the royal family*). We exchanged pleasantries and he gave me one *jin* of incense.

On the thirteenth day, we spent the night at Lạng Giang prefecture and met with the provincial magistrate Mr. Lê (*his name is Trinh. He has earned the title of palace graduate*) and the Fengyan County county deputy Mr. Phạm (*his name is Hanh, he earned the title cultivated talent*). I chatted and composed poems with each of them.

On the fourteenth day, we arrived at Cần Dinh garrison (*there is a garrison commander*). Near the outpost's border with Văn Giang county there is Câu Lậu lake, which produces cinnabar.[47]

On the fifteenth day, we spent the night at Quang Lang garrison. (*There were seven patrol stations between the Cần Dinh and Quang Lang garrisons; all were manned with guards.*)

On the sixteenth day, we traveled approximately three *li* and reached the Ghost Gate.[48] In the past, people used to say, "Of ten people who pass through the Ghost Gate, only one returns." Legend has it that there is a ghost market. In the afternoon, ghosts go through the gate and gather to engage in trade. If people offend them they will be struck with illness. As we rested beneath the gate, we felt a chill wind against our bodies, making our hair stand on end. Beside the gate there is a temple to the Wave-Quelling General [Ma Yuan] that is very efficacious (*every time envoys pass by they always offer incense in the temple*). Job's tears grows in front of the temple. (*It is what Ma Yuan took at that time to overcome the miasmic air and dispel toxins in the water.*[49] *People call it "qian and* kun *plant."*[50] *I gathered some and filled my bag.*) About two *li* to the southeast of the temple there is a rocky mountain that has a bronze pillar on it. (*There are two bronze pillars, the other one is in the Fenmao mountains in Qinzhou.*) It is one *zhang* [3.2 meters] tall and more than ten in width. It is the same color as the stones [on the mountain]. It is covered in bird shit. The local people say that weird creatures often sleep on top of it.[51] That night we slept in Artillery Battery Five. (*In the past when the governor of Bianzhou went on an expedition against the Tây Sơn rebels, he built eighteen artillery batteries between Lạng Sơn and Tongking all within sight of one another.*[52] *Now there are still names like "Battery Three" and "Battery Five."*)

On the seventeenth day, we arrived at the provincial capital of Lạng Sơn (*360* li *from Bắc Ninh*). South of Lạng Sơn all the way to Bắc Ninh is entirely desolate with narrow paths through the forest. Dense vegetation interlaced; hardy cogon grass grew taller than a *zhang*, filling our entire field of vision. There were very few homes, but empty mountains and deep valleys, as though still in primordial times. There was barely a sign that people had ever passed through, and cases of banditry were frequent. There were also rocky mountains dotted with tall peaks reaching into the empyrean. They were concealed by smoky miasma that did not disperse all day. Even in the spring, trees in the mountains were yellow and dried out. The rock was the color of iron, striated with moss. Streams flowed down from the summit where peacocks sometimes gathered to bathe. The intersecting branches of trees along the banks shaded the length of the streams, letting no sunlight through. Snakes and scorpions hid there, and their filth fell into the water; therefore the water's surface was the most poisonous. Travelers must wrap up their food supplies and dare not drink a drip of water from there. We had to heat Job's tears soup to have with our morning and evening meals. When travelers from far away come here, they find the eating habits most odd. As we approached Lạng Sơn, the mountain ranges became even closer together, [trailing off into the distance] like a massive meteor shower. There is a Coiled Serpent Mountain that is more than twenty *li* high. As we wound our way up, we switchbacked over dozens of peaks. When we were halfway up the ridge, we encountered an old gentleman with salt-and-pepper eyebrows. He was the county magistrate appointee Mr. Vũ (*his name was Huy Nhất, his style was Đường Trạch, he was a Provincial Graduate*) on his way to Cao Bằng Province. He was carrying a gourd of fine wine; and every two or three *li* he would squat on the ground and invite me to have a drink. This would turn into a spontaneous poetry session and a chance to forget my fatigue. Once we passed the ridge, he clasped his hands in parting, that grand old gentleman.

It was already afternoon when we reached the city. We met the provincial governor (*he was simultaneously in charge of Cao Bằng, so he was called the Lạng Bằng provincial governor*), Mr. Trần. (*His name was Văn Tuân. In the* renchen *year of the Daoguang reign [1832], along with Mr. Trần Văn Trung and Mr. Cao Hữu Dực, he had followed his king's command to go to Xiamen. After returning, he was rewarded with the title Grand Master for Excellent Counsel.*) When we walked through the door, the clerks were astonished, thinking we were important officials (*Vietnam does not have salaried students*). He [Mr. Trần] told me a topic, then he said, "A scholar from the Heavenly Court—even if only a student surely would still be talented and learned. Do not underestimate him." He was a large man with a handsome beard and mustache, with a youthful glow and white hair, gliding around like an immortal. He greeted us in the Chinese manner and talked about how he had a nice time with Zhou Yungao in Xiamen. When he heard that I was a student of Mr. Zhou, he was even more respectful, like he had never been happier in his life. He put me up in a guesthouse in the east of the city (*the proprietor Ou Bang was from Taiping in Guangxi*). He laid out a felt mattress. Everything was provided for us by the office, and a banquet was presented to us every day. He went on to notify Taiping Prefecture in order to request a date for us to go through the pass. (*The precedent: every time a person from the Heavenly Court was delivered by that country to the border, the provincial governor makes a report and then waits for Taiping Prefecture to send an official response setting a date to receive the person at the pass.*)

On the twentieth day, since he [Mr. Trần] knew I was lonesome, he wrote, "Lạng Sơn is the frontier and has often been ravaged by war (*three years earlier, the local people in Lạng Sơn and Cao Bằng had rebelled, and they had only been pacified since last year*), the towns were destroyed and hastily rebuilt.[53] When it comes to scenery or people, there is nothing to see. The only refined sightseeing destinations are a few grottos. You should try to experience them." He sent the clerk of the eighth rank Đoàn Văn Trung (*who could speak the Quanzhou dialect*) along with the market headmen from Guang[zhou] and Chao[zhou] to guide the tour.

From the city's east side, we crossed the stream and saw a rocky mountain to the northeast. Soaring up from level ground, it is called "The Mountain That Flew Here." Legend has it that Ma Yuan was about to build a fortification at the location of the mountain. When the foundation was laid, a mountain suddenly sprouted up overnight, so they moved the fortification to the west of the stream. Ma shot an arrow at this mountain; the arrow pierced the stone. Now the mountaintop is pierced with crevices just like it. After we had traveled about two *li* past the stream, we saw a region of rocky mountains. There were four connected peaks fused together with an amalgam of rocks. In front of the mountains there was a cave called Nhị Thanh. (*In the forty-first year of the Cảnh Hưng reign [1780] or jihai year, Lạng Sơn garrison had just been established by Ngô Thì Nhậm.[54] There had been a natural pattern on the rock that looked like the three characters* 二那青 *"two then green," and therefore the name of the cave is Nhị Thanh/"Two Green."*) There was a high wall made of bricks at the cave opening with three door panels in it. About twenty steps in the cave opened into a natural palace as wide as a square *mu*. The walls were all speckled with holes, lustrous and glistening like lamb fat. A stone base protruded from the center, like a lotus blossom stretching out of the water. In the base a statue of Confucius was carved. There were two smaller bases on either side. The one on the left was carved with Sakyamuni, and the one on the right with Laozi. It is called the Hall of the Three Teachings. (*Lê Hữu Dung wrote a record.*)[55] Pairs of stalactites hang down from the cave roof. Some look like bells, some look like chime stones, some look like small *ācārya* [preceptor] with the Anjali mudra [hands pressed together in prayer]. They are all the exact likenesses. There is a statue of the World Honored One [the Buddha] in the next cave. Then by winding along the edge we walked up into the last cave, where we passed through the north side of the mountain to Tam Thanh Cave.[56] It was so dark that we could not see a thing.

We exited the cave and walked a few steps to the right, crossed a small wooden bridge, and then explored another cave. The floor was broad, but the ceiling was narrow, like a bell. The floor was made of two flat sheets of rock that could hold dozens of people. Water was dripping and plinking all around, such that we forgot the sweltering heat of June. We lingered for a long time and then followed the face of the mountain for about two *li* until we arrived at Tam Thanh Cave (*opened in the forty-first year of the Cảnh Hưng reign [1780]*) which is wider than Nhị Thanh but not as curved. Inside, offerings are made to various heavenly bodhisattva statues, whose pearl and gem necklaces sent golden rays in all directions. Water without roots dripped down hanging stalactites from time to time.[57] Where it dripped it coagulated and patterned like stone. This was wonderful. There is a mountain facing the cave, with a single peak jutting out alone. It is called the "Awaiting Husband Mountain"; according to legend it is the place where Su Ruolan looked for Dou Tao, which is ridiculous.[58] When the sun was high in the sky, we looked for the old road to bring us back.

In the afternoon we went to the west side of the city and visited Đại Thanh.[59] (*I do not know when this one was carved out as there was no inscription to consult.*) The mountain path was steep and we had to pull ourselves up by vines and rocks, winding around several times before we reached the top. When we were about halfway up the mountain, the cave door was open a crack. There was a boulder that seemed poised to fall. Engraved on the wall were four large characters 石佛古跡, "Ancient Traces of Stone Buddha." We leapt into a magnificent realm. Inside an image of a bodhisattva had been made, solemn and stately. Its body and face had nothing strange. It was looking up with rapt attention as though the dust of this world were all empty, and the mind-nature was completely tranquil. Several paces behind the statue there was a hole that went to the top of the mountain that was dangerously narrow and hard to traverse. In front of the statue to the right there was a round hole. Ten paces past it one can see daylight. Our guide said that past this there was a cave that was even more secluded, and it was a pity that the sun was about to set and we were already footsore. So our tour of gorgeous scenery ended there. Truly it is an outstanding paradise abroad.

On the twenty-fourth day, the provincial governor arrived to offer sacrifices at the Temple of Literature. Officials and students all donned their official garb and held their tablets as they made their salutations. There were no sacrificial utensils prepared in the temple, no music and dance, only a flute and *huqin*, and the ceaseless ringing of bells. From the temple courtyard out they formed four lines oriented east to west, and strong soldiers held shields all around. Outside the gate they arranged two "fiery dragons." Once the sacrifice had ended, an official was sent to convey the roasted meat.

On the twenty-seventh day, we received a response from Mr. Jing (*Kun*) of Taiping Prefecture. (*He required us to arrive at the pass by the fifth day of the third month.*)

When Mr. Trần knew the travel plans, he arranged for a huge feast in the guesthouse on the twenty-eighth day. He ordered five civil and military officials to accompany me: the provincial magistrate of Trường Định prefecture, Mr. Đặng (*his name was Huy Thuật; he was a palace graduate*); the registrar, Mr. Nguyễn (*Đăng Giảng*); the department magistrate of Lộc Bình department, Mr. Nguyễn (*Đình Diêu*); the county magistrate of Văn Khai county, Mr. Hồ (*Văn Trước*); and the deputy guard, Mr. Nguyễn (*Kim Đôi*). When we were tipsy, Mr.

Đặng proposed that we take turns composing couplets or else quickly drain a big cup as forfeit. Mr. Đặng had a high tolerance for alcohol and nimbly composed verses that were powerful too. We all had a great time that day.

On the twenty-ninth day, I entered to thank Mr. Trần [Văn Trung], and we agreed that I would start my journey the next day. On hearing that I wanted to leave, he looked melancholy for a long time, and then took out ten *jin* [of silver] and several kinds of medicine as a gift. I turned down the money but kept the medicine and thanked him with a poem.

On the thirtieth day, I said farewell, and he sent the company commander of the sixth rank Nguyễn Văn Lương, the clerk of the sixth rank Đoàn Văn Trung, and two border pass officials Nguyễn Đình Tây and Nguyễn Hạng Kiểm, and others, along with twenty provincial soldiers, with crisp uniforms and shiny weapons, to escort us to the pass. He personally led this group of officials outside the city walls to see me off. He told me that when I returned to Xiamen I should tell Mr. Zhou Yungao that he recalled him fondly. He dared not send a letter because it was not appropriate to engage in foreign communication. Then we wiped away tears and clasped his hands in a farewell gesture. We crossed a stream and arrived at Khâu Lư market town. (*Traders from Guangdong and Guangxi and other places are allowed here.*) After thirty-five *li*, we arrived at Văn Uyên department.

On the first day of the third month, the department magistrate Mr. Nguyễn (*Diêu*) invited me to a banquet. That night, the border pass official Nguyễn Đình Tây also arranged a banquet for me.

The next day, the department clerk Trương Sùng Lễ and the stipendiary student Nong Mengqu (*he was from Ningming in Guangxi, and lived here as a guest*) all joined us bearing poems.

On the second day, the provincial magistrate Mr. Đặng [Huy Thuật] sent a poem after me, as well as two strings of cash. When he heard that, the department magistrate [Nguyễn Đình Diêu] also sent a poem and two strings of cash. I replied to them both with poems.

On the fifth day, we set out for Văn Uyên at dawn, coiling along small paths in and out of a jumble of mountains, where there was not the least sign of people or sound of chickens and dogs. We arrived at a defile after forty-five *li*. This was the South Pass. (*The Vietnamese call it the Oil Village Defile; it is at the border of Ningming Department, Taiping Prefecture in Guangxi Province. It forms the major crossroad of the border between Jiao [Vietnam] and Guang [Guangdong and Guangxi] and is defended by a squad leader.*) That day, the yamen of Zuojiang circuit, Mingjiang Subprefecture, and Ningming Department (*all near the South Pass*) all dispatched corvée soldiers from the barracks to collect me. I thanked my escort and bid them farewell and then headed north with the soldiers from Zuo River and the other places. From this time on, I left foreign soil and entered the Central Land. But when I recollect the earnest feelings of the Vietnamese officials and my countrymen living abroad, I cannot stop the tears that spring to my eyes.

When we first left the defile, there were very few residents, and the road was through rugged gorges, belonging to a mountainous frontier. After twenty-five *li* we rested at Xiashi (*place-name*) at Wenkou Hostel (*which is guarded by the staff of the Mingjiang office*), the proprietor, Mr. Sun (*his name was Beixiong, his style was Zijun, and he was from Jingui in Jiangsu. He was a descendant of Governor Sun Zhijun*) hosted me for a drink. Then we traveled another twenty *li* until we reached Shangshi department and spent the night at the office of the local department magistrate Mr. Bi (*Chengxiu, native from here*). (*The followers and corvée soldiers had food to eat that was provided by the office.*)

The next day, they moved the corvée soldiers to set out again (*the local department magistrate deployed them*), and at night we arrived at Ningming prefecture (*it is seventy li from Shangshi*).

On the seventh day, we met with the department chief of police, Mr. Lü (*Zhenlu, from Daxing county in Shuntian prefecture; the current department inspector and Wen Baogui had gone to the provincial capital on business; therefore, they deputized Mr. Lü*), and the advisor Mr. Jiang (*Xunxuan, from Jiangsu*) stayed to drink at the department office in the Blue Coral Studio. We engaged in intimate and cordial conversation until dusk, and then I retired.

The next day, departmental office staffer Mr. Yu (*Maodian, from Guangfeng county in Jiangxi, palace graduate of the* dingmao *year* [1807]) arrived to take up the post. I came to congratulate him and to request that he provide me with a long-form passport to avoid the hardship of seeking paperwork and messages along the road back to Min [Fujian].

On the ninth day, we received the papers and set off. After just over forty *li* we passed a small peak with a gate on top inscribed "Windswept Gate, Lofty Mountain." We traveled another four or five *li* and lodged at Wang Village.

On the tenth day, we arrived at the prefectural capital of Taiping (*it is 135 li from the department town of Ningming*) and lodged at Jingui Village (*located north from the town across a river*). The prefect Mr. Jing (*Kun*) had gone to the province on business at that time, so we were not able to meet.

On the eleventh day the rain prevented us from traveling. The next day it was still raining, so we braved the rain for four days until we reached Nanning prefectural capital (*it is 210 li from Taiping prefectural capital*) and lodged on Shuisha Street.[60]

On the eighteenth day, we rented a small boat from Nanning up the stream and passed through the Yongchun county seat in the evening. (*It is 200 li by boat from Nanning.*)

On the nineteenth day we descended the Sanzhou rapids. (*The route is entirely down rapids.*) There were many hidden rocks in the water, rather hazardous. At night we lodged at Hengzhou city. (*It is 160 li from Yongchun county seat by boat.*)

At daybreak on the twentieth day we traveled fifty *li* to Bantang Cliff. There was a temple on the riverbank where, according to legend, Emperor Jianwen of the Ming dynasty had lived.[61]

On the twenty-first day we arrived at Tantou station and visited the Temple of the Wave-Quelling General [Ma Yuan]. The temple had a majestic appearance, beneath a mountain and girdled by water, in the midst of a dark forest. An arch in front of the temple had four golden characters 伏波勝跡, "Magnificent Traces of the Wave-Queller." His spirit is very efficacious, and people who go down the rapids always visit the temple to burn ritual money. That day at noon, we went to Qijing rapids. The stream was as fast as arrows, and because of the rushing river, we could not move straight. The river was full of stones and obstacles on both sides, snaggled like dog teeth, and the boat had to navigate a narrow line between them, as if the boat and water were competing over the path. It was the most dangerous place of all. At sunset we anchored downstream from the Gui county seat. (*It is 180 li from Hengzhou city by boat.*)

On the twenty-second day we passed through the prefectural capital Xunzhou (*it is 190 li from the Gui county seat by boat*); in forty *li* we went down Tonggu rapids. The water flowed downward as though from a powerful waterfall. The boat floated down. Above the water we had to be aware of the checkered stones, while below the water we had to be aware of the mauve sandbanks. It was very dangerous.

On the twenty-third day, we passed through the Pingnan county seat (*it is 80 li from Xunzhou by the water route*) and went down the Jiangjun rapids. The high water surged past, churning torrentially. The boat scraped against boulders, which were spread as densely as stars, menacing us from all sides. At the very bottom there was a stone with an opening the size of a winnowing basket. If off by just a hair, we would be buried in the heart of the stone.

On the twenty-fourth day, we passed through the Teng county seat (*160 li from the Pingnan county seat by the water route*).

On the twenty-fifth day, we reached the Xima rapids at dawn. Once we passed this point, there were no more rapids. In the evening we passed through Wuzhou prefectural capital (*120 li from the Teng county seat by the water route*).

The next morning, we arrived at the Fengchuan county seat and crossed the border into Guangdong. (*It was subordinate to Zhaoqing Prefecture in Guangdong, 60 li from the Wuzhou prefectural capital by the water route.*) By sunset we were downstream of Deqing department (*100 li from the Fengchuan county seat by the water route*).

On the twenty-seventh day, we passed through Zhaoqing prefectural capital. (*It is 180 li from Deqing department by the water route.*)

Yuejiang Tower was along the bank. When we reached Longmen station, there was an Awaiting Husband Mountain. We passed the Sanshui county seat in the night. (*It is subordinate to Guangzhou Prefecture. It is 130 li from Zhaoqing prefectural city by the water route.*)

On the twenty-eighth day, we arrived at Foshan Town. (*It is 100 li from the Sanshui county seat by the water route.*) Foshan had attractive scenery, gorgeous people, rich merchants, and flowing merchandise. Its markets and shops were second only to Yangcheng [Guangzhou]. Three days previously, the Xi River had suddenly risen (*the water comes from Guangxi, so it is called the Xi or "west" River*), and the water in front of people's houses had risen to three or four *chi*. I rode a small boat through the market. It was like entering a valley of ten thousand flowers—more than the eye could take in! Seventy *li* from there is the Guangdong provincial capital. (*It is called "City of the Five Goats." To the south of the city is Fuxu Town and the harbor.*) The water route from Nanning to here is approximately 1,700 *li* or more. It was all smooth sailing, though we passed through sixty-eight rapids, all of them along the border of western Guangdong. The mountains along the river were dried out and not green. It drizzled incessantly. When we did see mountains, cities, or remote markets, they were quiet. In the clouds and mist, only Nanning and Wuzhou differed from the other places in having some hubbub. After we passed Zhaoqing, the landscape was more lovely, the scenery became more beautiful, the markets and towns more bustling, and very lively. It could be called a fertile land.

On the twenty-ninth day, we met with the salt commissioner, Mr. Zheng (*Kaixi, style name Yunlu. He was from Longxi in Fujian*). We chatted about our native place at great length, and he did not ask me about my experiences on my journey.

On the first day of the fourth month, I went to Yingxiang Street (*outside of Jinghai Gate*) to visit my friend Lin Boliao (*from Longxi in Fujian*) and chanced upon Du Guangji (*Tamsui, Taiwan*), a person from the same prefecture as me. He had brought along his friends Chen Tianyou and Cai Jie (*they were both from Xiamen, Fujian*) to invite me to enter the city. Then we visited the Shrine of the Five Goats together.

(Legend has it that when the city was being built, five old people appeared, then suddenly turned into five goats and disappeared. The people thought they were immortals, so they named their city after the five goats and built a shrine to worship them.) Then we climbed Guanyin Mountain. *(It is to the north of the city and is the highest point, so it serves as the city's garrison.)* When we arrived in front of the Guanyin Temple *(the temple is at the top of the mountain)*, we saw the roof tiles of the city's buildings spread out as numerous as scales on a fish, and towers, temples, pagodas standing out distinctly before our eyes. Beyond the city, mountains surrounded all sides, abundant water swirled around, sparse woods standing in the distance, interlaced with hazy mist. The stupas towered in a row at the river's mouth. *(There were Stupas One, Two, and Three.)* The mountains of Xiangshan and Macao seemed close enough to touch.[62] I exclaimed about this grand view of mountains and the sea of the south. We entered the temple, performed a prostration, and went out. To the east we passed the Tower of Five Mirrors *(the tower has five stories. It is more than twenty zhang [64 meters] tall)*, then went to the shrine of Mr. Zheng *(the place where Anqi Sheng became an immortal.[63] Now there is a shrine there)*. We passed through the Cry of the Wind Pavilion and the Jade Mountains Villa, turned to exit through the Penglai Palace. *(These are all places where officials and gentry occasionally come to relax and hold banquets.)* Curving railings, finely wrought windows, flowering arbors—such tranquility that it seemed as though the world of immortals had suddenly sprung up from the dust of the mundane world. In the evening we went to the market and saw precious, lovely, and colorful objects spread out and valuable foreign commodities piled up like mountains. At dusk we went to Fuxu Town *(south of the city)*. There the sound of flutes roiled the water, the boats were full of singing and dancing, and the reflection from candles and light from lamps illuminated the river from top to bottom. Poets and wealthy customers vied with one another on board the magnolia boats.

The next day we crossed to the south of the river and visited Hoi Tong Monastery *(near the river's south bank)*. Shayuan is along the bank; this village has so much jasmine it is like entering a realm of perfume. Turning around one sees the Pearl of the Sea Stone (*there is a temple called Cidu Temple; it is also called Pearl of the Sea Temple*) spurting out from the waves. Passing ships often go around it. At noon on the dot when the sun was beating down, an unexpected breeze from the river ruffled my face and clothes, hot and cold rapidly fluctuating. It was the way a person's life flashes before the eyes like fireworks, becoming nothing but a trace. Although I was enjoying myself, how could I get so attached to this place that I forgot about returning [home]? Then I took my fellow travelers back to our lodging, anxiously setting a time to return.

On the fourth day, Du Guangjin lent me twenty *jin*. I hired a cargo ship from Shi Jun again (*he is from Jinjiang county in Fujian*) that would take us to Laolong (*the name of a place in Longchuan county [Guangdong]*). We took our leave of several people and then immediately boarded the ship.

On the seventh day we passed the Boluo county seat. (*It is under the administration of Huizhou Prefecture; it is three hundred and ten li from the provincial capital by the water route. The town encircled the Hulu mountain.*) We saw Luofu Mountain. (*The saying goes, "In Huizhou they cannot see Luofu above, in Guangzhou they cannot see Luofu below."*)[64] In the evening we passed Huizhou prefectural capital. (*Huizhou has two cities, one for the provincial military commander and one for the provincial magistrate. It is thirty-five li from the Boluo county seat by the water route.*) Siwu Mountain, White Crane Grotto, Wujiang Pavilion, and [Wang] Zhaoyun Mausoleum are notable sites in the city; all were established when Dongpo [Su Shi] was here.[65] We crossed a stream east of the city and were in the Guishan county seat.

On the twelfth day we passed through the Longchuan county seat. (*It is four hundred and forty-seven li from the Huizhou prefectural capital by the water route.*) Five *li* south of the town is Ghost Tower. According to legend there are many ancient graves there. Back when the county seat was established here, a bunch of ghosts created problems by stealing all the peoples' bricks in the night and building a tower, so the town had to be moved elsewhere. The tower is ugly and leans to the side, but it never fell down. Thirty-five *li* by boat from the county seat, we arrived at Laolong. It is more than eight hundred *li* from Goat City [Guangzhou] to Laolong. The nine days on the boat were all scorching hot and unbearably stuffy. Fortunately Lin Huishan (*from Longxi*) and Ding Gongchen (*from Jinjiang*) were fellow passengers that passed the time joking and chatting with me. Gongchen was well versed in astronomy. He had sailed to Luzon [in the Philippines] (*a foreign island to the southeast*) to trade and stayed there for several years and learned methods for measuring the heavens from Westerners. His textual criticism of it was also very proficient. He tirelessly discussed astronomy with me daily, instructing me about his maps of the earth and tools for measuring the heavens. In general, it set the equator, ecliptic, northern zone, and southern zones as the Western methods did. It used the horizon to measure the distance between the center of the earth and the north or south poles.[66] This method was based on the technique of the armillary sphere, but with quicker and easier measurement. I questioned him in detail, thinking about practicing this another day, in order to prove to the experts that I did not neglect the benefit of my boatmate's teaching.

On the thirteenth day, we came ashore at Laolong. It was thirty *li* to Qinling and then another twenty *li* to Languan; this is the road that one must take to get from Guangzhou to Chaozhou. At the top of the pass there is a shrine to Duke Wen of Han [Han Yu]; when Duke Zhao (*Shenzhen*) was inspecting Guangdong, he had it repaired and made like new.[67] Upon entering the shrine, I saw a lifelike statue of a deity, and I lingered to gaze at it in reverence before I resumed my journey. Ten *li* later we arrived at Qiling at sunset. We hired a small boat to carry us night and day in order to make haste.

On the fifteenth day, we arrived at the Three Rivers Dam at dawn. (*It is three hundred and thirty-four* li *from Qiling.*) The water takes three paths at this place: one [branch] goes to Dabu, one to Chaozhou, and one to Qiling. That is why it is called Three Rivers. There is a small town on the bank where we were stopped for an inspection. There is a very noisy market outside the town. In the evening we arrived at the county seat of Dabu County. (*It is under the jurisdiction of Chaozhou*

Prefecture. It is one hundred and seventy li from Three Rivers Dam. We had to anchor the boat two li from the town.)

On the sixteenth day we went ashore at Dabu. In the afternoon, once we reached the border of Yongding County, we then crossed into my home, Min [Fujian] (*under the jurisdiction of Tingzhou prefecture*).

On the seventeenth day, we reached the border of Nanjing County (*under the jurisdiction of Zhangzhou prefecture*), on the other side of the Tianling Mountains. When we reached the mountains, first we wound around the edge on a narrow path, switchbacking for five or six *li*, and it was not that arduous. But once we had traveled about two *li* up the face of the mountain, we looked up after every step, as though we were scaling a stairway to heaven. The sedan bearers were gasping for breath. When we descended the peak, we hurried straight down from the ridge, hurtling down more than three thousand steps before the terrain started to level out. Glancing down made me feel like I would fall, so I was too terrified to look. We came to a river just over twenty *li* past the mountain and boarded a small boat. We arrived at Guanxi on the afternoon of the second day. (*It is also called Xiaoxi. We took the lesser route from Dabu to here, so I cannot count the mileage in detail.*) I noted that from Guanxi to the south, the two counties of Hui[zhou] and Chao[zhou] were divided by high mountain ranges and deep valleys, crisscrossed by peaks and rivers. The people lived in *tulou* surrounded by mountains, secluding their dwellings in the rugged mountains where it is easy to conceal evildoing.[68] They had to clear mountain forests to cultivate their fields because there is little open country for farmland. It is also far away from the sea, so they cannot benefit from fishing and salt cultivation. Both men and women serve as porters and traders. The people are poor and their ways are rough—this is due to their situation.

From Guanxi we rented a night boat and arrived at the Zhangzhou prefectural capital at dawn on the nineteenth day. (*It is one hundred and fifty-two li by the water route from Guanxi.*) Then we went east to the prefectural office and climbed Zhi Mountain to the north, looking for traces of the former sage [Zhu Xi].[69] However, they were submerged by the passage of time, and there was no so-called Pavilion of Awe.[70] Only an old shrine to him remained at the foot of the mountain. I bowed before the shrine, went to the southern part of the city, and spent the night within the south gate.

On the twentieth day, we went out the south gate and found a boat to go from the tributary river to the sea. The wind was with us, and we made it to Xiamen that night. On the twenty-second day, I met my teacher circuit intendant, Zhou Yungao, who felt like I had been reborn. He said that I must have seen and heard many strange things on this journey. He said, "You have already written 'A Record of Peril'; you should also write a 'Travelogue.' And when you return one day to Taiyang [Tainan], you can use it to tell your friends and family [about your experience]."

On the second day of the fifth month, I boarded an oceangoing ship. On the eighth I returned to Penghu. My brother, Tingyang, and I bowed to our mother in front of the main hall. Surprised and happy, she shed a lot of tears. Reminiscing about the past, it really did feel like I was reborn.

As for this trip, I could not count how much we had traveled by sea. From when we set out from Quảng Ngải on the twenty-first day of the twelfth month in the *yiwei* year [February 7, 1836] to when we reached Xiamen on the twentieth day of the fourth month of the *bingshen* year [June 3, 1836] took 42 travel days on land, traversing 3,300 *li*. We took 33 travel days by water, traversing 3,374 *li*. Because we lingered on the way, the whole journey by land and sea took 118 days in total. Despite enduring difficult roads and islands, I completed this epic journey. Since my good fortune is heaven's will, I documented it in detail.

~~~~~~

Master Yungao's commentary: He kept notes contemporaneously, taking inspiration from the dwellings and rare sights. The style is based on Li Xizhi's *Register of Coming South* (*Lan Nan lu*) and Gui Xifu's *Travelogue of the Renxu Year* (*Renxu jicheng*) but with more feeling of lushness. The parts depicting the sights in the work partially come from Liu Liuzhou's *Record of Mountains and Rivers* (*Shanshui ji*).

Vietnam is what was called Việt Thường [Ch. Yuechang] in ancient times. It is in the South Sea, reachable from Taiwan by sea in eighty-three watches.[1] The ocean is to the east of the landmass [of Vietnam], various barbarians are to the west (*Laos and other places*), Champa is to the south. (*Champa was a separate country. It was once called Nhật Nam. During the Ming, the Lê absorbed it.*) To the north it borders Sien prefecture in Guangxi and Lin'an Prefecture in Yunnan. What was called Nhật Nam in the past is now Quảng Nam; it is known as Tây Kinh. What was called Giao Chỉ in the past is now called Annam; it is known as Đông Kinh.[2] Now they are united as one country.

In the time of Tang and Yu, it was known as Nam Giao.[3] During the Qin dynasty [221–206 BCE] it was Elephant commandery. At the beginning of the Han dynasty [202 BCE—220 CE], Zhao Tuo occupied it. [Emperor] Wu pacified Nam Việt [Ch. Nanyue; the kingdom founded by Zhao Tuo] and established Giao Chỉ commandery [in 111 BCE]. During Emperor Guangwu's reign [25–57 CE], the women Trưng Trắc and Trưng Nhị rebelled. Ma Yuan pacified them and erected bronze pillars to mark the border. During the Jian'an reign period [196–220 CE], the name was changed to Giao Province. In the Tang dynasty [618–907] it was changed to Annam, and a military governor for the Peaceful Sea Army was established. It all belonged to the Central Land [China]. Later it was abandoned due to frequent uprisings, but tribute was received. During the Five Dynasties period [907–79], the local person Khúc Thừa Mỹ usurped power and [the territory] was annexed by the Southern Han dynasty [917–71]. At the beginning of the Song dynasty [960–1279], Đinh Liễn [940–79] possessed it and was granted the title King of Giao Chỉ. Đinh Liễn's [family's rule] lasted three generations, after which it was usurped by Lê Hoàn [941–1005]. The Lê family lasted for three generations; the throne was usurped by an official, Lý Công Uẩn [974–1028]. The Lý family lasted for eight generations. When there was no longer an heir, the throne was passed to the son-in-law, Trần Nhật Cảnh [1218–77]. The Yuan dynasty [1271–1368] conquered them and made his son Quang Nhuế the king of Annam commandery.[4]

At the beginning of the Hongwu reign of the Ming dynasty [1368–98], the Ming crowned Trần Nhật Khuê as king of Annam; at that time, [Annam] invaded Champa. After four generations, the throne was usurped by an official, Lê Quý Ly, who executed all of the Trần descendants. During the first year of the Yongle reign [1403], the Lê son Hồ Đê was crowned king.[5] The next year, [Trần] Nhật Khuê's son Thiêm Bình and the official Bùi Bá Kỳ knelt before the palace requesting vengeance. The emperor ordered that he be welcomed back as ruler of his country. The Lê duplicitously killed Thiêm Bình and the troops accompanying him. Subsequently, [the Ming] dispatched troops to launch a pincer assault. They captured the father and son. The search for Trần heirs was not successful, so [the Ming] incorporated the land as prefectures and counties. They established fourteen prefectures, forty-seven departments, one hundred and fifty-seven counties, and twelve guards and installed three offices to govern it. Later Trần Giản Định and his son [Trần] Quý Khoáng wreaked havoc one after the other; once they were pacified, Lê Lợi launched another rebellion. In the second year of the Xuande reign [1426], Lợi dispatched a messenger requesting that Trần Cảo be made king. Yang Shiqi and Yang Rongyi called a ceasefire and recognized him, dismissing the three offices. Cảo died and Lợi duplicitously claimed that the Trần line was extinguished. The emperor permitted him to take charge of state affairs. His son Lân inherited his recognition as king and annexed Champa. After ten generations, the throne was usurped by an official, Mạc Đăng Dung. In the sixteenth year of the Jiajing reign [1537], Đăng Dung was terrified because the prince Lê Ninh came [to Beijing] and requested an army. He surrendered and pledged loyalty [to the Ming], and his position was changed to commander-in-chief of Annam [demoted from king]. The Lê clan were resettled at Tất Mã River. The Mạc continued to pass on the throne until they were chased out by Lê Ninh's son [Lê] Duy Đàm. The emperor appointed Duy Đàm as commander-in-chief, and the Mạc were settled in Cao Bằng, following the precedent of the Tất Mã River resettlement. During the fourth year of the Tianqi reign [1624], the Lê attacked Cao Bằng, and the Mạc were further weakened. Up until the fall of the Ming the two families divided the territory.

During the fifth year of the Kangxi reign of our dynasty [1666], Lê Duy Hy was recognized as the king of Annam.[6] In the fifty-fourth year of the Qianlong reign [1789], the Lê clan lost the country. [Nguyễn] Quang Bình was recognized as king of Annam.[7] In the seventh year of the Jiaqing reign [1802], the title king of Annam was changed to king of Vietnam, because the name of the country had changed from Annam to Vietnam.[8] Their historical records detail the information, so I will not venture to redundantly give more details. I, Tinglan, only heard about recent events while on the road and could not verify them in detail. Along with what I saw firsthand, this book will provide for discussion of what is happening abroad for now.

According to what people who have been to Vietnam say, at the end of the Lê period the country was in chaos. The country was divided in three. Gia Long (*the reign name of the father of the current king, surname Nguyễn.*[9] *It is the biggest taboo for the people of the country to mention the kings' names*) occupied Lũng Nại (*now Gia Định Province*).[10] Thái Đức (*I am not sure of his surname; the term here is his reign name*) occupied Tân Châu (*now Bình Định*).[11] Quang Trung (*I am not sure of his name. Originally he was a merchant from the hamlet of Tây Sơn. He called himself the king of Tây Sơn, and others called him the Tây Sơn rebel. And he illegitimately took the reign name Quang Trung*) occupied Thuận Hóa [Huế] (*now Phú Xuân*).[12] They each ruled their region and became sworn brothers.[13] When Thái Đức died, his son was threatened by officials and fled to the protection of Quang Trung. Quang Trung plotted to kill him and seize his kingdom. Angered by this, Gia Long raised an army to attack him and took over Tân Châu city, leaving his son-in-law to defend it.[14] Quang Trung dispatched his junior mentor and grand minister of the masses to encircle Tân Châu city with troops.[15] There was a stalemate for several years until he sent the commander-in-chief with reinforcements. They ran out of food within the city. The reinforcements were exhausted from their long trip. (*From Tân Châu it takes eleven days to go north to Thuận Hóa and more than twenty days to go south to Lũng Nại.*) They lost several battles, and the city fell. Gia Long's son-in-law self-immolated.[16] The commander-in-chief moved the troops to Lũng Nại. Gia Long's troops were disbanded and fled to the ocean. Strengthened, Quang Trung annexed Đông Kinh and replaced the Lê king. When Gia Long fled to the ocean, the pirate He Xianwen (*a Cantonese*) surrounded him with several hundred ships.[17] Gia Long was running out of options. In distress, he devised a plan: he came out on the deck of the ship, put on his crown, and shouted, "I am the king of Lũng Nại! Now my state has been destroyed, so I am going to seek troops from other countries to exact vengeance. We have nothing onboard, so there is no benefit to harming us. But if we join together and help each other to destroy our enemy, on the day of victory I will share the state with you and make you a king." Delighted, Xianwen pledged his loyalty. They went together to Siam and requested several tens of thousands of elite troops, launched a pincer attack, seized Lũng Nại and Tân Châu, took advantage of their momentum to capture Thuận Hóa, and then pushed on to Đông Kinh. Quang Trung escaped to the mountains with his remaining troops.[18] His junior mentor and grand minister of the masses went to Đông Kinh by obscure routes and were captured by hidden troops. Gia Long waxed them into torches and burned them as a sacrifice to his son-in-law. Đông Kinh also fell to him. All of Annam was his.

He changed the name of Lũng Nại to Gia Định ["Auspiciously Settled" 嘉定] and the name of Đông Kinh to Thăng Long ["Ascending Prosperity" 升隆].[19] He changed the reign name to Gia Long ["Auspicious Prosperity" 嘉隆], because he started in Gia Định and succeeded in Thăng Long. Once his reign was established, he dispatched an envoy to present tribute to the Heavenly Court and request that his title be changed to king of Vietnam. He cut a prefecture out of his territory and gave it to Xianwen. Xianwen could not dare resist [so he took the prefecture]. But because he lacked supporters, the local people did not accept him, and they eventually left. Gia Long was grateful to him, so he always treated Tang people generously. The current king [Minh Mạng] succeeded to the throne more than ten years ago and bestows even more favors than in the past. Traveling merchants are safe there.

Later, a general of Gia Định rebelled.[20] Four prefectures were taken in one day. Many foreigners followed him. The king sent troops that surrounded it for several years, losing more than fifty thousand soldiers (*many were crushed to death by battle logs on the city walls*). The residents of Gia Định knew that the king had had a rift with Siam. (*Siam had previously committed troops to help Gia Long take the country, and every year, hundreds of people went back and forth to that country to serve as replacements for those performing military service. But later, because they could not stand the maltreatment, they all fled back to their country. Substitutes were not sent, and good relations ceased.*) They secretly sent a letter entreating the king of Siam, who therefore dispatched a navy one hundred thousand strong to help them, with Tang people as their local guides. When they were about to arrive at the city, [the guides] stole all the gold and fled. The navy got lost, and the Vietnamese government army intercepted and killed more than half of them. The [Siamese soldiers] retreated in defeat. Those within the city were without help, and the large army attacked them even more fiercely; they built outer walls, spied into the city from them, and used cannons to surround and fire on it. After another fifteen days, the city fell and was completely annihilated.

In the *renchen* year (*the twelfth year of the Daoguang reign in our dynasty*) [1832], a local bandit from Cao Bằng rebelled, joining with refugees in a border town in Guangxi.[21] They ganged up and destroyed Cao Bằng city and then spread to Lạng Sơn. They created unrest for two years before they were put down. Since this, their king is more wary of Tang people, but he does not know that the chief instigators were all local people.[22] There were only one or two foreigners among them who were cunning and took the opportunity to secretly attach themselves to them or were coerced into it against their will, but then, as a result, tens of thousands of migrants lost the favor and gained the enmity of the king, and even traders were subjected to higher taxes. Is it not unjust?

After the Tây Sơn rebel Quang Trung entered the mountains, he ruled the savages and assembled his gang to raid and plunder. He still referred to himself as "the king of Tây Sơn." His son and grandson continued this. (*Cảnh Thịnh and Bảo Điển were their spurious reign names.*)[23]

There was also a kind of Snake Demon Savage who belongs to the White Miao. It lives in the mountains and reproduces a lot. They are governed by a Snake Demon King. Sometimes they band together and go out to kill people.

When I, Tinglan, surreptitiously observed the circumstances of Vietnam, [I saw that] their royal city was solid and prepared [for defense]. They were sheltered by mountains and sea. They could claim sovereignty based on their geographical location. From north to south [the territory] is like a long rope, more than five thousand *li* long and all under their control. They are not concerned about annexation, so it truly is a great one among the foreign vassals. What they should worry about is that the whip won't reach [the belly of the horse]; the people's customs are degenerate and inconstant.[24]

The current king [Minh Mạng] respectfully serves the Heavenly Court [which] deeply illuminates the way of governing [for him]. He is especially well versed in writings and history (*he ordered the printing of his own collected works of poetry and literature*), he respects the learning of the classics (*high officials have mostly taken the imperial examination*). He serves his mother in order for people to hear of his filial piety and saves money (*the treasury is filled with gold and silver*). He is good at making money and engaged in commerce everywhere. If any country has something that [Vietnam] does not have, he will import it. When it comes to a skill, he is sure to spread the techniques. Although the clothing follows the old system, standards fully comply with the system in China (*such as in recruiting officials, reviewing officials, documents, and legal precedents, there is no difference with China*). The king once said, "When it comes to what the Heavenly Court respects, among all those who comply with the morality of a vassal, the various barbarians [beside Vietnam] are not worth mentioning." There has been no break in tribute missions up to the present. Chinese officials and scholars who have been blown off course and landed here have all been treated well.

Their king makes a tour once or twice during the first month of every year. Sometimes he is carried in a sedan chair, sometimes he rides a horse or an elephant, [outfitted] with gorgeous attire and exquisite weapons, and [accompanied by] a thousand armed soldiers. When he passes by markets and stores, households line up altars to welcome him. He bestows three strings of cash on each to demonstrate his exquisite courtesy. When he has no business to attend to, he often stays in the palace. There are more than a hundred princes who live in other palaces. Some study civil matters, and others study the military arts. They have a quota for food, and if they break rules, then their allotment will be decreased. If anyone from the royal family, their affines, and below uses their influence to bully people, even if they are relatives of the king, they must be punished according to the law.

The ranks and names of their civil service inside and outside the court follows the system of the Heavenly Court. In the past, those who became officials were all from the families of government clerks. The clerks outside the nine ranks of official position move up according to vacancy. Now the examinations are more important. There is one examination held every three years, and the officials of learning enforcement are requested to come up with examination questions. Child candidates need to go to their provincial capital to be tested on literature and art, essays and the classics, and prose and poetry. The most outstanding ones win the Provincial Graduate title, while those who are acceptable become cultivated talents. Cultivated talents who are over forty years old are selected as teachers, while provincial graduates are selected as county magistrates. Those who have not taken up a post should take the metropolitan examination. If they pass, they become palace graduates. The king personally chooses staff for the Hàn Lâm Academy and to fill in for county magistrates from the palace examination. There is no title from the palace examination.[25] Their military positions follow the country's old system; there is no examination. Although the salary of office holders is low, those who manage lawsuits do not dare accept bribes. Criminals are prosecuted very harshly, [so] even high officials like the provincial administration commissioner and surveillance commissioner have not accumulated a lot of money. They usually do not wear hats or shoes, their feet are bare, whether meeting the commoners or the king. Those who have achieved merit are granted a belt and shoes. When they enter the royal hall, they are allowed to wear crimson slippers (*nicknamed "slides"*).

Only during important ceremonies do they wear the apparel accorded to their rank: the court dress, tablet, boots, and headgear of the Han system. Some people have two shoulder bags (*shaped like a purse but bigger*) to store all of their writing implements and provisions in. Those with official posts carry it on their person. They open a dark green waxed canopy when they come and go (*they use a big umbrella to make the canopy*); they do not distinguish color. Those who achieve merit are granted an extra layer of the canopy. It is a great honor to have several layers of canopies. "Wheels" are always carried by two people, no matter the social rank of the rider. (*A "wheel" is a sedan chair. It is made of one strip of bamboo. The bottom is made of silk netting held together at the two ends with horizontal crossbeams. Two turtle-shell-shaped bamboo-leaf cushions are on the two ends enclosed by reed mats. Someone enters the seat by opening the reed mats from the side and laying down on the cushion. Officials use wooden strips colored in red. Those at rank three or above have red and the rest have blue or black.*)[26] They are guided by ten strong soldiers, each carrying just a rifle, a wooden baton, a sword, and several pairs of rattan ropes.

The soldiers do not belong to specific generals. There is a set number of [soldiers] attached to the yamens of civil officials according to their hierarchies. The ones supplied to provincial [yamens] are called provincial troops. They wear bamboo helmets (*the helmets are so small that they barely cover their heads*) that are painted gold with a chicken feather stuck in it. Their uniforms are red serge with green margins and green sleeves. At the prefectural and county levels, they are called prefectural troops or county troops, and their helmets are painted green or black, with a chicken feather in it. Their uniforms are made of black cloth with red hems and red sleeves.[27] Their weapons are of the highest quality, but the country produces no iron and very little gunpowder. (*They frequently drill by just going through the motions without firing them.*) Ordinary soldiers are unskilled and weak. Since military law is so strict, just before a battle they will still proceed even if it means certain death. In leading troops, their commanders especially use schemes to luck into victory. The people submit or rebel depending on whether an army would succeed. Therefore disorder breaks out easily when people come into contact with or depart from [the government], and kindness and trust are not enough to solidify [the loyalty] of the people.

The instruments of punishment used to control people are rattan switches, long cangues, handcuffs, execution, and military exile.[28] When it comes to capital punishment and banishment, they observe the legal precedents of the Heavenly Court to set punishments without exception. The arm of the law is long. When criminals hear that the constable has arrived they turn themselves in. They use one strand of rattan to bind together several hundred people and none dare to flee.

Their villages each have a village chief and neighborhood chiefs. When there is an issue they hit a wooden clapper. If there are robberies in the village, the village chief will hit the clapper three times in a row. The neighboring villages will hit their clappers in response, and people will come out from every corner of the village to apprehend [the robbers]. No one can escape. When they capture robbers, they need the stolen goods as proof. If they are caught outside of the house and do not have stolen property on them they let it go, therefore, there are many petty robberies. When people fight, regardless of whether it is men or women, if no one wants to budge, then they fall to the ground and do not get up, then they call that "lying down."[29] (*The first one to get up is said to have the weaker case.*) Even if their relatives are strong, they do not dare to help. When the village chief hears about it, he will strike the clapper to gather a group of people to mediate. If they cannot resolve it, then he will allow a lawsuit to be filed at the government office. The injured party will be moved to lie down at their enemy's house, moaning and groaning night and day without eating. The officials would pressure the enemy to cure the victim and then handle the litigation. Because of this people tend not to fight and rarely beat others to death. They especially do not assault pregnant women. (*If a pregnant woman is beaten and injured, the punishment is doubled.*) In cases of adultery, whether the woman is already married or not will be taken into consideration. (*When an unmarried woman engages in illicit sex, if the woman agrees, the official will order them to marry, but if the woman is already married, the perpetrators will be beheaded.*) There are no brothels. Smoking opium is strictly prohibited; those who sell it and those who smoke it are sentenced to death and their family property seized by the government. They do not stop people from gambling. There are drifters who do it for a living, and even more migrants are addicted to it. There are those that gamble away a mound [of money] and draw one another into bad habits, and although the culture deteriorates, officials do not look into this. It is worrisome. They are also forced to pay excessive taxes. (*For local people, each family member must pay twelve strings of cash in taxes every year. For Tang people, the amount is reduced by half.*) Every seven people need to support the food of one soldier. The people from the hinterlands are lazy and do not do much in the way of livelihood. Even the rich ones have less than ten thousand pieces of gold, and the poor ones make a living by portering and selling firewood.

Tigers cause a lot of problems in the mountains. One can often see a crowd of firewood gatherers presenting a tiger to an important official, who then gives them five strings of cash. They release the tiger and then snare it in a net, remove its teeth and claws, and take it to the military training ground.[30] They drive a herd of elephants in, and the tiger roars.

The elephants then yield—pissing and shitting themselves. Only an old elephant will charge straight at the tiger and drive it into a corner to fight. The tiger will then fall to the ground without moving. Then the herd of elephants will jostle each other trying to trample the tiger, which will be crushed to meat in no time. I asked why they do this and was told, "To provoke the elephants, so that they will no longer be afraid of tigers." Elephants are really strong and they can understand what people say. Each provincial office raises a dozen or more, and they engage in military exercises twice a year. (*Every time the elephants are inspected, first the troops are lined up in formation, the elephants are driven into the formation, straw men are made to put into the front line, and the elephants will stretch out their trunks to attack them, immediately breaking the straw men. Only lighting a fire will make them evade.*) They are called the Strike Force, and they are hard to beat. (*The method of resisting elephants, as recorded in the* History of the Ming: *In the fourth year of the Yongle reign [1406], when Zhang Fu defeated Annam, he encountered elephants with torches tied to their tails. [The Chinese] painted lions onto their charging horses to deceive them, making the elephants retreat.*) Although these beasts are fierce, they are not as reliable as people.

I made a close study of their popular customs. Although many Han descendants live there, they have gotten mixed up with the ancient customs of the Yi and Liao. They are devious and stingy, and one should not get close with them. Men flit around gambling and relaxing and they sit around at home waiting to be fed. In domestic affairs, they heed their wives. They like to wear black tunics, red trousers, and bamboo rain hats (*shaped like an upside-down cauldron*). When they meet people, they doff their hats to bow their heads and clasp their hands to show respect. Their clothes are worn out, unwashed, and full of lice which they pick and chew on. They call it "sucking in your own life essence." (*This applies to the rich and poor alike. When officials are meeting with the people, they loosen their clothes to hunt for lice, and no one thinks it is weird.*) They love bathing, and even in the winter months they will pour cold water from the crowns of their heads to their feet. Married women go out to engage in trade with their hair tied up and their feet bare. They use silk crepe headbands to tie on flat bamboo hats and wear narrow-sleeved red-and-black thin silk clothes that hang down low. Their jewelry is jade, pearls, or agate prayer beads or copper or metal bracelets. They do not wear skirts or apply cosmetics. All food products and groceries are carried to the market and then laid on the ground. They call this "the line-up." (*There are two a day, called the morning market and the evening market.*) The markets are crammed with products. Their tea, medicine, porcelain, used clothing, and other goods are mostly imported by ship from China.

When men and women get married, the betrothal money is not fixed (*it can be as little as ten strings of cash*). When the time comes, the groom goes to the bride's house with the matchmaker to fetch her. (*The bride walks with her husband; she does not use a palanquin or horse.*) Female members of the two households accompany the bride, but without lanterns or music. If a woman leaves her husband, she must give back the betrothal money. Women like to take Tang people as their husbands and call them *chú* [uncle].[31] The custom is that sons and daughters inherit property equally. When they make sacrifices to the ancestors, they must simultaneously offer sacrifices to the wife's parents. They do not make the sacrificial tablet. They write couplets to paste on the walls of the hall and light incense there. Spirits sacrificed to by the household are called Bản Đầu Công (*it is like the Earth Lord of Fujianese people in China*). In the main hall, they offer sacrifices to the Mysterious Lady of the Nine Heavens.[32] (*They put up a tall wooden board and display a shrine in front of it to place the incense. Below it they plant a lot of palm lily and different kinds of lovely flowers.*) They have memorial tablets for the spirits in their temples, not carved statues. To welcome the spirits, one person will perform a song, while people alongside strike drums (*sometimes four people*), without other instruments. When they enter a temple, they light countless firecrackers for good luck.

The people mostly live in thatched huts (*because tiles, bricks, and mortar are expensive*). The center is high, and the four sides are low. They hang a bamboo curtain in front of the room to block the door, and they raise it during the daytime. Their dwelling places have no tables and chairs; they make low beds where they hang out night and day. They do not make bedding; when it is cold they just wrap themselves with mats. Only Chinese people who have emigrated there to live and wealthy people have built houses with roof tiles and high gates, and many tools. They are called "great family compounds." They serve their food and drink on a copper tray (*without the copper tray, it is considered rude*). They set it on the mat, with meat dishes and delicacies arranged on it. Their alcohol is very strong and they serve it cold. They eat beef, pork, and fish half raw (*they do not cook meat because they think it is delicious when it is uncooked and bloody; each morsel is very small, just enough to grab with the chopsticks*). They arrange several overlapping large plates, usually with cut up fresh lettuce and various greens, with salty fish sauce to eat it with. (*Their cooking pots are made of copper; they call them mộc khẩu, so they eat a lot of fresh lettuce and greens to disperse the poison from the copper.*[33] *They also do not use soy sauce; they use fish sauce instead. It is very pungent.*) When they are done eating, they use their hands to wash their faces. (*They do not use washcloths.*) Then a person will bring out a round bamboo basket with Thuận Hóa tea on it. (*Thuận Hóa is the location of the royal seat; nowadays it is called Phú Xuân. The tea that is grown there can disperse the poison from copper vessels. It can also allay summer heat. It is bitter and astringent.*) They use slips of paper to roll up tobacco leaves, then light them and inhale. (*They do not use water pipes.*) They often chew betel, and many have black teeth.

When there is an opportunity to celebrate something, they put on a play and have fun. Once, on the road out of Thường Tín, I saw the owner of an inn who raised a troupe of pretty boys and beautiful women who could perform *zaju* operas.[34] Guests at the inn could pool together two strings of cash and invite them to demonstrate their skills. The actors painted their faces with red ink, wore short jackets with narrow sleeves, socks but no shoes. They jumped and spun around in Deva-māra dance, stretching their fists and kicking their legs, slapping their thighs and staging fight scenes, following the beat of a gong.[35]

They then change to unmade-up faces, wearing brocade robes, and perform the story of the former lord [Liu Bei, 161–223 CE] of Shu [one of the Three Kingdoms] bidding farewell to Xu Yuanzhi [Xu Shu, ca. second century CE].[36] They alternated slow and fast rhythms, mournful melodies, with the troupe master playing along on the flute, the *huqin* fiddle, or drums for the songs. Soon after, four girls came out standing shoulder to shoulder, their slender waists swaying to tiny steps, and danced and sang with their arms linked. Their exquisite beauty was so seductive. When the song ended, they knelt and bowed with their hands pressed together before their foreheads to express their gratitude.

There was another time, in Lạng Sơn, when I saw an old woman plucking a mouth harp. (*It is shaped like a common* yueqin *lute, but with a very long handle, four strings, and sound that was quiet and distant.*) Two girls in dazzling attire came out to sing along. They sang together in a low key, the melancholy sound lingering. As soon as each song ended, they started talking to each other in murmurs, and I could not understand them.[37] They could also perform a sinuous dance, gracefully advancing and retreating, charmingly pirouetting while bending low. If people tossed them coins they would cast amorous side glances and smile enchantingly. Although this is a foreign custom, it has its own special characteristics. People often invite [performers like them] to entertain while they are drinking. If there are one or two people who can sing Chinese songs, they are especially favored by people.

Their spirit mediums, medical practitioners, diviners, and mathematicians are all Tang people. When a ship arrives everyone is ready. Of the places Chinese ships congregate, Gia Định Province (*Lũng Nại*) is the most popular. Next [most popular] is Quảng Nam Province (*Hội An*), and then Bình Định Province (*Tân Châu*) and Quảng Ngãi, then Phú Xuân (*Thuận Hóa*), Nam Định (*commonly called Bi Phỏng*), Nghệ An and other provinces. The liveliness of the market, taxes, and the amount of the gifts for the officials all depend on the size and number of the ships. Ships arrive in the winter and depart in the summer. It is commonly said, "When the peacock moves on, the Tang ships arrive;

when the '*suhe/Tô Hòa*' calls, the Tang ships depart." (*In the past there was a stepmother who gave birth to a son called Suhe. Because of some trouble he escaped to Annam and did not come back. The next year, the mother sent her stepson to look for him. When he arrived in Annam, his inquiries about his brother came to nothing. Not daring to return home, he died of illness and his soul transformed into a bird that calls "Suhe" everywhere. At the time when the Tang ships are about to leave, its mournful call is especially numerous, therefore they call it the "Suhe bird." Nowadays this bird is really common, and its call really sounds just like "Suhe.*")

For the past several years, officials have forbidden the private export of cinnamon, raw sugar, and other commodities; set official prices; authorized the royal house to trade [these goods]; and increased the taxes on merchant ships. Because of this, Chinese ships are increasingly rare, down by forty or fifty percent, and the people are very resentful about it. In Hà Nội (*formerly Đông Kinh*), Bình Thuận (*formerly Champa, within its borders is Flame Mountain. Once summer has started, the ground is as hot as fire, and one cannot walk there in the daytime without being burned up. Therefore there is no human trace during the daytime*), and other provinces, all the ships are small and local ones and most of the goods are Cantonese. There are ships called "nha tử" ships. (*The big ones can carry more than two hundred piculs. According to* Records of Taiwan Prefecture (Taiwan jun zhi), *in the fifty-sixth year of the Kangxi reign period [1717], a small warship held together with rattan was blown to Penghu by a storm—it is precisely this kind of ship.*) The bottom of the boats is made with woven bamboo strips, and the outside is painted with coconut oil; only the deck of the boat is made of wood. The small ones are all like this. There are also ones with wooden bottoms, with rattan woven through it closely to hold it together.[38] If water gets in, they bail it out with a wooden ladle from time to time. (*They have no iron there, so they make their small boats without any nails at all.* Record of Things Heard and Seen in the Maritime Kingdoms *says: "Woven boats have no stern or prow; if they are inundated with water, they put closely woven lashings at the bottom and the deck of the boat and use several hundred oars to tow it from a distance. If their ship runs aground, Western ships are terrified of running into these woven ships of Quảng Nam." They are perhaps the nha tử ships.*)[39] Generally speaking, in places that are adjacent to the coast, they prefer to have a lot of masted ships converging together with lots of money and goods circulating. Otherwise, there will be poor and unemployed people who will die in the ditches.

Farmers do not fertilize the fields (*because they do not dare to eat vegetables that have been covered in filth*), nor do they use well sweeps to transport water (*because they do not have wooden barrels for home use, they use ceramic containers to draw water*). When there is a drought, they allow the sprouts to naturally wither. They do not distinguish between early and late rice paddy, they just continually harvest and reap. In the highlands, they plant millet and peanuts (*also called "tudou"*), and to a lesser extent they grow sweet potatoes, but no sorghum, beans, or wheat.[40] Their local products include gold and pearls, tortoiseshell, coral, rare hardwoods, aromatic woods, incense, cinnamon, ebony, sappan wood, pepper, styrax benzoin, antelope horn, ivory, rhinoceroses and tigers, apes, baboons, peacocks, silver pheasants, tree kingfishers, boas, ant eggs, jackfruit, cane sugar, coconut oil, peanut oil, potato vine, betel nut, cotton, homespun cloth, crepe, patterned silk, finespun, mother-of-pearl inlays, and other products.

The land is divided into thirty-two provinces: Phú Xuân (*the location of the royal palace*), Quảng Nam, Quảng Ngāi, Bình Định, Phú Yên, Cao Miên [in present-day Cambodia], Khánh Hòa, Bình Thuận, Biên Hòa, Gia Định, Hà Tiên, An Giang, Định Tường, Vĩnh Long, Quảng Trị, Quảng Bình, Nghệ An, Hà Tĩnh, Thanh Hóa, Ninh Bình, Nam Định, Hưng Yên, Hưng Hóa, Sơn Tây, Tuyên Quang, Hà Nội, Hải Dương, Thái Nguyên, Bắc Ninh, Quảng Yên, Lạng Sơn, and Cao Bằng. It is somewhat more than five thousand *li* from north to south, but not even forty *li* across, all stretched out along the coast. Only the two provinces of Hà Nội and Gia Định have large territories and bountiful products. (*Hà Nội produces many luxury items; Gia Định produces a lot of rice, paper mulberry, sugar, and oil.*) Besides these two provinces, the goods produced by Vietnam do not surpass those produced by a single Chinese prefecture. Once you enter the interior mountains of the southwest, then it is all high ridges and remote forests. These mountains extend for several thousands of miles without a trace of human beings. Only [the legendary walkers] [Da] Zhang and [Shu] Hai could ever penetrate it.[41]

I, Tinglan, through the peril of wind and wave, journeyed in a foreign land. Although the details were lost in translation, I fortunately encountered many émigrés from my home province and was able to visit them and ask them about things everywhere I went and learned that our dynasty's enlightening influence can make even the most wild locales look eagerly toward civilization. China and foreign countries are truly one family. I was gifted the resources I needed to return to my home soil. How could it not be that the sagely Son of Heaven's lofty generosity gave rise to this? I am therefore offering my limited observations of my expedition, chronicled here in outline.

~~~~~~

Master [Zhou] Yungao's commentary: When writing of foreign places, he accurately records things as they happened, and the ethos of the foreign people is apparent. Through his ups and downs there, he completely rose to the occasion, and this is what we call being appropriate.

POSTSCRIPT ONE

Above is what Cai "Source of Fragrance" [Cai Tinglan] wrote: One part is called "Record of Peril on the High Seas," which narrates the misfortunes of the ship and the people on it and how they traveled at night and barely survived; the next part is "Travelogue of the Fiery Wasteland," which narrates Cai's journey from danger to safety and the experiences on his trip back; the final part is "Vietnam Chronicle," which takes up [Vietnamese] institutions, clothes and goods, and customs in order to show that the extent of [our] country's enlightening influence has no limit.

Previously, rumor had it that Mr. Cai would never return from this trip. I visited Mr. Liu Cibai [Liu Hong'ao, 1778–1849], and he told me, "Mr. Cai is cultivated in morality and is good at writing.[1] He is full of ambition, talent, and knowledge. He has not been able to fulfill his aspiration with officialdom, and on top of it all, now he has run into this predicament. This cannot be the will of heaven!" Later, the less news we got, the more people talked. I reflected that there were many cases from antiquity to the present in which talented and outstanding people, ranging from Lingjun [Qu Yuan] to Wang Zian [Wang Bo] and Li Gongfen [Li Bai] were not tolerated by creation and were submerged beneath the waves.[2] Therefore, I did not think it would necessarily not be the case.

Now, as Mr. Liu predicted, Mr. Cai has returned! After visiting his parent, he then came to visit my residence. I asked for a summary. Since spoken words could not fully describe it, after several days, he copied what he had written and brought it to me. I increasingly believed that Cai benefited from this situation, in which he encountered difficulties, but the gods did not forsake him. He is nothing like those boasters or profiteers. It is [thus] proper that even while struggling in a barbaric country, every place he went was like a homecoming.

As for his "Vietnam Chronicle," it all came from what he saw, heard, and checked in historical documents. Unlike local annals or records of exotic places, everything in his record is based on evidence and is trustworthy.[3] His eagerness to learn was not interrupted by the predicaments among the barbarians. I know that since that time, his morality has become more solid and writing more outstanding. If one day he takes a position in the court, he would certainly be able to stand independently, equalizing disasters and happiness and unifying life and death. It is not by accident that heaven drove him to danger and made him travel ten thousand *li* on water and land! Since Mr. Bai wrote a preface to the book, I thus attached a few words to return to Mr. Cai.

Magistrate of Taiwan Prefecture and friend, Xiong Yiben
AUGUST 27, 1836

POSTSCRIPT TWO

In the past, I read the accounts of various foreign countries in Chancellor Ye of Futang's [Ye Xianggao, 1559–1627] *Cerulean Cloud Collection* (*Cangxia Ji*), which included biographies and discussions. Annam was the only country in the southeast [included in the text]. Starting from the time of Yao and Shun, all the way to Han, Tang, Song, Yuan, and Ming, it listed the imperial lineages, narrated rebellion and conquest, and occasionally touched on local customs. The chancellor had never been to Annam. During the Ming dynasty, while the families of Mạc, Lê, and Trân competed for the throne, the Ming first took Annam and administered it as their territory and then later abandoned it. As they say:

> The great troops were thrice dispatched
> And they were thoroughly outmatched.
> Maybe the court did not think it through,
> but then there was nothing they could do.

The chancellor heard stories and consulted historical records and therefore used it as a warning.

Now, Mr. "Source of Fragrance" [Cai Tinglan] of Penghu entered the sea from Heron Island [Ludao]. The sailors did not read the winds correctly and catastrophically ran into the storm, drifting ten days to arrive in Annam. No matter their social status, southerners welcomed [Cai], accommodated him, and asked for his poetry and calligraphy. After more than a month, he learned that two routes from Yunnan and Guangxi led to China and then asked to enter Guangxi from their country. He then crossed into Guangdong and arrived at the Tingzhang Imperial Circuit. He returned to Heron Island and went home from there. Traveling on a boat and returning on land, the trip lasted more than four months. He wrote the three chapters "Record of Peril on the High Seas," the "Travelogue of the Fiery Wasteland," and "Vietnam Chronicle."

Mr. Cai entered the raging seas with loyalty and trustworthiness, treading through danger as though it were flat ground, and the gods did not forsake him. This has already been fully addressed in the prefaces by the circuit intendant and the prefect.[1] He left tracks from the royal capital to the border. His interviews and translations were extremely detailed and thorough. Does this not exceed merely filling in some gaps in the historical records? Annam has great reverence toward our dynasty. Since the royal Nguyễn family held the country, they knocked on the pass and paid tribute since the beginning years of the Jiajing reign [1522–66]. The current king especially follows his duty as a subject. This is tremendously different from the previous dynasty [the Ming], which was neither able to pacify or appease them, failing in taking and abandoning. It is a historian's convention to record the general ideas of local buildings and customs. As he traveled, Mr. Cai also wrote down an overview of the topography, the positive and negative aspects of their practices, and the merits and demerits of their governance. Based on where he went and what he discovered and published, is it just empty words on paper?

Ye Wenzhong [Ye Xianggao] was a famous official of a vanquished county [the previous dynasty]. His book was more comprehensive than previous histories. Mr. Cai's record is even more comprehensive than the *Cerulean Cloud* and is closer to the recent situation. He used his firsthand experiences to generate his analyses. People who read this collection will get a good sense of how Mr. Cai could assist the governance of the dynasty someday.

The Previous Tingzhou Prefecture school superintendent,
and your humble brother, Ke Longzhang

GLOSSARY

Entries below are arranged by English translation used in text, characters, pinyin transliteration, and/or *quốc ngữ* transliteration. We have chosen not to transliterate into *quốc ngữ* those terms that only appear in the text in an exclusively Chinese context. Vietnamese word order differs from Chinese word order; for example, *garrison commander* in Vietnamese would be *quan đồn thú* rather than *đồn thú quan*. Below, we have transliterated terms using Han-Viet word order rather than writing words to reflect colloquial Vietnamese, so that readers can match the characters to their pronunciations.

ABBREVIATIONS

Ch   Chinese
V   Vietnamese

ADMINISTRATIVE UNITS

county 縣 xian (Ch) huyện (V)
county seat 縣城 xiancheng (Ch) huyện thành (V)
department 州 zhou (Ch) châu (V)
prefecture 府 fu (Ch) phủ (V); 郡 jun (Ch) (V) (unofficial way to refer to fu 府 in Qing)

prefectural capital 府城 fucheng (Ch) phủ thành (V)
province 省 sheng (Ch) tỉnh (V)
station 汛 xun (Ch) tấn (V)
subprefecture 廳 ting (Ch) sảnh (V)

BOOK TITLES

Cerulean Cloud Collection 蒼霞集 *Cangxia ji* (Ch), by Ye Xianggao 葉向高

Miscellany of the South Seas 海南雜著 *Hainan zaju* (Ch) *Hải Nam tạp trứ* (V), by Cai Tinglan 蔡廷蘭

Record of Mountains and Rivers 山水記 *Shanshui ji* (Ch), by Liu Zongyuan 柳宗元

Record of Things Heard and Seen in the Maritime Kingdoms 海國聞見錄 *Haiguo wenjian lu* (Ch), by Chen Lunjiong 陳倫炯

Records of Taiwan Prefecture 台灣郡志 *Taiwan jun zhi* (Ch)

Register of Coming South 來南錄 *Lai Nan lu* (Ch), by Li Ao 李翱

Travelogue of the Renxu Year 壬戌記程 *Renxu jicheng* (Ch), by Gui Xifu 歸熙甫

TERMS

association, confraternity 幫 bang (Ch, V)

Bản Đầu Công (V) 本頭公 Bentou Gong (Ch)

battery 炮台 paotai (Ch)

Black Ditch 黑溝 Heigou (Ch)

Blackwater Ocean 黑水洋 Heishui yang (Ch)

brush talks 筆談 bitan (Ch) bút đàm (V)

Central Land 中土 Zhongtu (Ch)

child student 童生 tongsheng (Ch)

Chinese people 中國人 Zhongguoren (Ch)

Chinese speech 華語 Huayu (Ch)

cultivated talent 秀才 xiucai (Ch) tú tài (V), another name for licentiate 生員 shengyuan (Ch)

earth 地中 dizhong (Ch)

Earth Lord 土地公 Tudi Gong (Ch)

earthen buildings 土樓 tulou (Ch)

Fujian native-place lodge 福建鄉祠 Fujian xiangci (Ch), sometimes known as 會館 huiguan (Ch) hội quán (V)

great family compounds 大家圍 dajia wei (Ch)

Hakka 客家 Kejia (Ch) Khách gia (V)

Heavenly Court 天朝 Tianchao (Ch) Thiên Triều (V)

horizon 地平 diping (Ch)

Imperial College 國子監 Guozijian (Ch) Quốc tử giám (V)

inner sea 內洋 neiyang (Ch)

lineup 排行棧 paihangzhan (Ch)

metropolitan examination 會試 huishi (Ch) hội thi (V)

Min tongue 閩音 Minyin (Ch)

Minh hương (V) 明香/明鄉, Ming xiang (Ch); literally, "Ming incense" and "Ming hometown"

nha tử ship (V) 牙仔船

Official Language 官話 Guanhua (Ch)

One Thousand Li Stone Embankment 千里石塘 Qianlishitang (Ch) Thiên Lý Thạch Đường (V)

optimus 狀元 zhuangyuan (Ch) trạng nguyên (V)

outer sea 外洋 waiyang (Ch)

palace examination 殿試 dianshi (Ch) thi đình (V)

palace graduate 進士 jinshi (Ch)
tiến sĩ (V); literally, "advanced
scholar"

People of the Heavenly Court 天朝人
Tianchaoren (Ch)

potato vine 薯榔藤 shulangteng (Ch)
thự lang đằng (V)

provincial exams 鄉試 xiangshi (Ch)
hương thi (V)

Provincial Graduate 舉人 juren (Ch)
cử nhân (V), literally, "recommended man"

Qing people 清人 Qingren (Ch)
Thanh nhân (V)

secundus 榜眼 bangyan (Ch) bảng
nhãn (V)

slides 淺拖 qiantuo (Ch) thiển đà /
dép lê (V)

strike force 衝鋒軍 chongfengjun
(Ch) quân xung kích (V)

Tang people 唐人 Tangren (Ch)
Đường nhân (V)

Ten Thousand Li Sandy Shoal 萬里
長沙 Wanlichangsha (Ch) Vạn Lý
Trường Sa (V)

tertius 探花 tanhua (Ch) thản hoa
(V)

Yuyuan's personal blocks 郁園藏板
Yuyuan cangban (Ch)

PLACE-NAMES (VIETNAMESE)

An Giang 安江

Annam (V); Annan (Ch) 安南

Awaiting Husband Mountain, Vọng
Phu sơn / núi Vọng Phu 望夫山

Bắc Ninh 北寧

Bi Phỏng 碑放

Biên Hóa 邊和

Bình Định 平定

Bình Thuận 平順

Cẩn Dinh 芹營

Cao Bằng 高平

Cao Miên 高綿

Câu Lậu lake 勾漏海

Champa, Chiêm Thành 占城

Chợ Luân 幣崙

Chợ Ròn 浡市

Cố Luân 固崙

Cù Mông 虬蒙 mistake for Chính
Mông, referring to Quảng Ngãi
City

Định Tường 定祥

Đồng Nhân 同仁

Elephant commandery,
tượng quận 象郡

Gia Định 嘉定

Giao Chỉ 交趾

Hà Hoa 河華

Hà Nội (Hanoi) 河內

Hà Tiên 河仙

Hà Tĩnh 河靜

Hải Dương 海陽

Hưng Hóa 興化

Hưng Yên 興安

Khẩn Bản 緊板

Khánh Hóa 慶和

Khâu Lư 駈驢

Lạng Sơn 諒山

Lộ Vạn 潞澗

Lộc Bình 祿平

Lý Nhân 里仁

Lũng Nại 隴奈

Mountain that Flew Here, Phi Lai
    Sơn/núi Phi Lai 飛來山

Nam Định 南定

Nam Giao 南交

Nhật Nam 日南

Ninh Bình 寧平

Nghệ An 乂安

Nghênh Hạ 迎賀

Nguyệt Đức River 月德江

Nhị Hà River 珥河江

Oil Village Defile, Du Thôn ải
    油村隘

Phú Xuân 富春 [Huế]

Phú Yên 富安

Quảng Bình 廣平

Quang Lang 桄榔

Quảng Nam 廣南

Quảng Ngãi 廣義

Quảng Trị 廣治

Quảng Yên 廣安

Sơn Tây 山西

Tân Châu 新州 equivalent
    to Bình Định

Tất Mã River; aka Mã River 漆馬江

Thái Nguyên 太原

Thăng Long 昇隆

Thanh Hóa 清華

Thới Cần 菜芹

Thuận Hóa 順化 [Huế]

Thường Tín 常信

Trung Cố 中固

Trường Định 長定

Từ Sơn 慈山

Tuyên Quang 宣光

Two Green Cave, Nhị Thanh
    二青洞

Việt Thường (V) Yuechang (Ch)
    越裳

Vạn market 帮潤

Văn Uyên 文淵

Vĩnh Long 永隆

PLACE-NAMES (CHINESE)

Awaiting Husband Mountain,
    Wangfu Shan 望夫山

Bantang Cliff 迤塘岩

Boluo 博羅

Changtai 長泰

Chaozhou 潮州

Chongwen Academy 崇文書院

Dabu 大埔

Dehua 德化

Deqing 德慶

Fengcheng 豐城

Fengchuan county seat 封川縣城

Foshan 佛山

Fuxu Town 扶胥鎮

Guangdong 廣東

Guangzhou 廣州

Guangxi 廣西

Guanxi 管溪

Guanyin Temple 觀音寺

Gui County 貴縣

Guishan 歸善

Hengzhou 橫州

Heron Island, Ludao 鷺島

Hoi Tong Monastery 海幢寺

Huizhou 惠州

Hulu Mountain 葫蘆山

Jiangjun Rapids 將軍灘

Jinjiang County 晉江縣

Jinmen 金門

Laolong 老隆

Lin'an 臨安

Longchuan 龍川

Longxi 龍溪

Macau 澳門

Mingjiang Subprefecture 明江分府

Nanjing County 南靖縣

Nanning 南寧

Nan'aoqi 南奧氣

Pearl of the Sea Stone, Haizhu shi 海
珠石

Penghu 澎湖

Pingnan county seat 平南縣城

Qijing Rapids 起敬灘

Quanzhou 泉州

Sanshui 三水

Sanzhou Rapids 三洲灘

Shayuan 沙園

Shrine of the Five Goats, Wuyang Ci
五羊祠

Sien Prefecture 思恩府

Taiping 太平

Tamsui 淡水

Tantou station 灘頭汛

Teng county seat 藤縣城

Three Rivers Dam 三河壩

Tong'an 同安

Tonggu Rapids 銅鼓灘

Wuzhou 梧州

Wuzhouyu 浯洲嶼

Xiajiang County 峽江

Xiamen 廈門

Xingquan Yong Circuit, Xingquan
Yongdao 興泉永道

Xiashi 下石

Xiangshan 香山

Xima rapids 洗馬灘

Xunzhou 潯州

Yangcheng 羊城

Yongchun county seat 永淳縣城

Yuejiang Tower, Yuejiang Lou 閱江樓

Zhangzhou 漳州

Zhao'an County 詔安縣

Zhaoqing Prefecture 肇慶府

OFFICIAL TITLES

assistant envoy 副使 fushi (Ch)
phụ sứ (V)

associate administrator 同知 tongzhi
(Ch)

association headman 幫長 bangzhang
(Ch) bang trưởng (V)

border pass official 守隘官 shouai
guan (Ch) thủ ải quan (V)

circuit intendant 觀察 guancha (Ch)

clerk 書吏 shuli (Ch) thư lại (V)

coast guard official 汛官 xunguan
(Ch) đồn quan chức cửa tấn (V)

commander-in-chief 都統使
dutongshi (Ch) đô thống sứ (V)

company commander 該隊官 gaidu-
iguan (Ch) cai đội quan (V)

county deputy 縣丞 xiancheng (Ch)
huyện thừ (V)

county magistrate 知縣 zhixian (Ch)
tri huyện (V)

county magistrate appointee 候補知
縣官 houbu zhixian guan (Ch)
hầu bì tri huyện quan (V)

department chief of police 州吏目 zhoulimu (Ch) châu lại mục (V)

department clerk 州書吏 zhoushuli (Ch) châu thư lại (V)

department magistrate 知州 zhizhou (Ch) tri châu (V)

department office 州署 zhoushu (Ch)

deputy guard 副衛官 fuweiguan (Ch) phó vệ quan (V)

director of the Ministry of Revenue 戶部郎中 hubu langzhong (Ch) hộ bộ lang trung (V)

director of the Ministry of Works 工部郎中 gongbu langzhong (Ch) công bộ lang trung (V)

district magistrate 縣令 xianling (Ch) huyện lệnh (V)

envoy 行人 xingren (Ch) hành nhân (V)

examiner 考官 kaoguan (Ch) khảo quan (V)

garrison commander 官鎮 quan trấn (V)

garrison commander 屯(守)官 Tun (shou) guan (Ch) đồn thú quan (V)

garrison commander 鎮兵官 zhenbing guan (Ch) trấn binh quan (V); 總兵 zongbing (Ch) tổng binh (V)

governor 省堂官 shengtangguan (Ch) tỉnh đường quan (V)

governor-general 總督官 zongduguan (Ch) tổng đốc quan (V)

Grand Master for Excellent Counsel 嘉議大夫 Jiayi dafu (Ch) Gia Nghị đại phu (V)

grand minister of the masses 大司徒 dasitu (Ch) Đại tư đồ (V)

grand secretary of the East Hall 東閣大學士 dongge daxueshi (Ch) đông các đại học sĩ (V)

guard 衛 wei (Ch) vệ (V)

guard official 守禦官 shouyuguan (Ch) thủ ngự quan (V)

guards 屯員 tunyuan (Ch) đồn viên

Hanlin Academy 翰林 Hanlin (Ch) Hàn Lâm (V)

inspector 刺史 cishi (Ch)

instructor 教諭 jiaoyu (Ch) giáo dụ (V); 教授官 jiaoshouguan (Ch) giáo thụ quan (V)

interpreter 通言 tongyan (Ch) thông ngôn (V)

junior mentor 少傅 shaofu (Ch) thiếu phó (V)

leader of a thousand 千總 qianzong (Ch)

lecturer 主講 zhujiang (Ch)

local magistrate 通判 tongpan (Ch) thông phán (V)

market headman 庯長 buzhang (Ch) phố trưởng (V)

military governor 節度使 jiedushi (Ch) tiết độ sứ (V)

minister of personnel 吏部尚書 libu shangsu (Ch) lại bộ thượng thư (V)

native chieftain 土司 tusi (Ch) thổ ty (V)

official of learning enforcement 督學官 duxueguan (Ch) đốc học quan (V)

patrol station 汛防 xunfang (Ch) đồn (quan) phòng (V)

Peaceful Sea Army 靜海軍 Jinghaijun (Ch) Tĩnh Hải Quân (V)

prefect 府尹 fuyin (Ch) phủ doãn (V); 太守 taishou (Ch)

prefectural governor 府堂官 futangguan (Ch) phủ đường quan (V)

prefectural office 府署 fushu (Ch)

provincial administration commissioner 布政官 buzhengguan (Ch) bố chính quan (V); 藩 fan (Ch) phiên (V)

provincial governor 巡撫/ 巡撫官 xunfuguan (Ch) tuần phủ quan (V); 府堂官 futangguan (Ch), another way to refer to zhifu 知府

provincial magistrate 知府 zhifu (Ch) tri phủ (V)

provincial military commander 提督 tidu (Ch)

registrar 經歷 jingli (Ch) kinh lịch (V)

squad leader 把總 bazong (Ch) bả tổng (V)

staffer 屬員 shuyuan (Ch) thuộc viên (V)

stipendiary student 廩生 linsheng (Ch) lúm sinh (V)

surveillance commissioner 按察官 anchaguan (Ch) án sát quan (V); 臬 nie (Ch) niết (V)

vice director of the Ministry of Rites 禮部員外郎 libu yuanwailang (Ch) lễ bộ viên ngoại lang (V)

vice prefect 府丞 fucheng (Ch) phủ thừa (V)

PEOPLE

Bảo Điển 寶典 (reign name)

Bùi Bá Kỳ 裴伯耆

Bùi Hữu Trực 裴有直

Bùi Kính Thúc 裴敬叔

Cai Jie 蔡節

Cai Peihua 蔡培華

Cai Tinglan (Ch) Thái Đình Lan (V) 蔡廷蘭

Cai Tingyang 蔡廷揚

Cảnh Thịnh 景盛 (reign name)

Cao Hữu Dực 高有翼

Chen Qi 陳棨

Chen Tianyou 陳天佑

Đặng Huy Thuật 鄧輝述

Đặng Kim Giám 鄧金鑑

Ding Hongchen 丁拱辰

Đinh Liễn 丁璉

Đoàn Văn Trung 段文忠

Du Guangji 杜光己

Fan Chengda 范成大

Gia Long 嘉隆 (reign name)

Hồ Đê 胡杏; aka Hồ Hán Thương 胡漢蒼

Hồ Văn Trước 胡文著

Hoàng Văn 黃文

Hồ Bảo Định 胡寶定

Jiang Xunxuan 江遜軒

Jiang Yi'an 蔣懌莘

Jing Kun 景錕

Khúc Thừa Mỹ 曲承美

Kuang Lu 鄺露

Lê Duy Đàm 黎維潭

Lê Duy Hy 黎維禧; aka Lê Huyền Tông

Lê Hoàn 黎桓

Lê Hữu Dung 黎有容

Lê Lân 黎麟; aka Lê Thái Tông

Lê Lợi 黎利

Lê Ninh 黎寧

Lê Quý Ly 黎季犛; aka Hồ
    Quý Ly

Lê Tĩnh Uyên 黎靜淵

Lê Triều Quý 黎朝貴

Lê Trinh 黎楨

Li Bai 李白

Li Zhenqing 李振青

Lin Boliao 林伯僚

Lin Huishan 林回山

Liu Bei 劉備

Liu Hong'ao 劉鴻翱

Liu Zongyuan 柳宗元

Lu Jia 陸賈

Lü Zhenlu 呂振鷺

Lý Công Uẩn 李公蘊 aka
    Lý Thái Tổ

Mạc Đăng Dung 莫登庸

Ngô Thì Nhậm 吳時任

Nguyễn Bạch 阮帛

Nguyễn Đăng Giảng 阮登講

Nguyễn Đăng Uẩn 阮登蘊

Nguyễn Diêu 阮眺

Nguyễn Đình Diêu 阮廷姚

Nguyễn Đình Tây 阮廷西

Nguyễn Hạng Kiểm 阮行儉

Nguyễn Nhược Sơn 阮若山

Nguyễn Nhược Thủy 阮若水

Nguyễn Quang Bình 阮光平 aka
    Nguyễn Huệ

Nguyễn Sĩ Long 阮仕龍

Nguyễn Tiến Thống 阮進統

Nguyễn Văn Lương 阮文良

Nong Mengqu 農孟區

Ông Ích Khiêm 翁益謙

Phạm Hanh 範亨

Phạm Hoa Trình 範公華程

Phan Thanh Giản 潘清簡

Qu Yuan 屈原

Quan Nhân Phủ 關仁甫

Shi Jun 施均

Source of Fragrance 香祖 Xiangzu
    (Ch) Hương Tổ (V) (Cai Tin-
    glan's style name)

Su Shi 蘇軾

Sun Beixiong 孫倍雄

Thái Đức 泰德 a.k.a. Nguyễn Nhạc

Trần Cảo 陳暠

Trần Giản Định 陳簡定

Trần Hải Đình 陳海亭

Trần Hưng Trí 陳興智

Trần Nhật Cảnh 陳日煚; a.k.a. Trần
    Thái Tông

Trần Nhật Khuê 陳日煃; a.k.a. Trần
    Dụ Tông

Trần Quang Nhuế 陳光暠; mistake
    for 陳晃

Trần Quý Khoáng 陳季擴

Trần Thiêm Bình 陳天平; in Viet-
    namese records, written 陳添平

Trần Văn Trung 陳文忠

Trần Văn Tuân 陳文恂

Trịnh Đức Hưng 鄭德興

Trưng Nhị 徵貳

Trưng Trắc 徵側

Trương Sùng Lễ 張崇禮

Wang Bo 王勃

Wang Kunyuan 王坤元

Wen Baogui 聞寶桂

Wong4 Bik1 Gwong1 黃壁光 Hoàng
    Bích Quang

Wu Yanghao 吳養浩

Xu Jinping 許蔭坪
Xu Shu 徐庶
Xu Xiake 徐霞客
Vũ Huy Nhất 武輝一
Vũ Văn Dũng 武文勇
Yang Rongyi 楊榮議
Yang Shiqi 楊士奇
Ye Xianggao 葉向高

Yu Maodian 俞懋典
Zheng Kaixi 鄭開禧
Zhou Kai 周凱; a.k.a. Zhou Yungao
　周芸皋
Zhu Jian 祝艦
Zhao Shenzhen 趙慎軫
Zhao Tuo (Ch) Triệu Đà (V) 趙陀

WEIGHTS AND MEASURES (CHINESE)

fang 方 and dou 斗 (1 fang = 4 dou = 1 liter)
li 里 = 576 meters
zhang 丈 = 3.2 meters
chi 尺 = 0.32 meter
cun 寸 = 0.032 meter
liang 兩 = 37.3 grams

guan 貫 = a string of cash
gong 弓 = 23,040 meters
wei 圍 = the length between one's thumb and the index finger of the same hand
mu 畝 = 414 m^2

HOKKIEN TERMS

chhut-hái 出海　captain
hàkim 下金　part that fastens the rudder
kahpán 甲板　name for foreign boats

phâng 篷　sail
sêngkài 檻蓋　walls and ceiling of cabin

HOKKIEN/TEOCHEW NAMES

Cheng Thi/Thiam 曾添　Tăng Thiêm (V)
Chia Kì 成記　Thành Ký (V)
Chiok Lām 祝艦　Chúc Hạm (V)
Hô Êng 胡榮　Hồ Vinh (V)
Hông Kín 洪謹　Hồng Cẩn (V)
Hông Liâng 洪涼　Hồng Lương (V)
Hông Tèng 洪錠　Hồng Định (V)

Iông/Yeoh Ban Kì 楊萬記　Dương Vạn Ký (V)
Lim Khiám 林懍　Lâm Khiểm (V)
Lim Sàng 林送　Lâm Tống (V)
Lim Sùn 林遜　Lâm Tốn (V)
Ng (or Hông) Bun 黃文　Hoàng Văn (V)
Ngô Sim 吳深　Ngô Thâm (V)

Ông Chhit 王七　Vương Thất (V)　　Sím Lim 沈林　Thẩm Lâm (V)
Sím Jim 沈壬　Thẩm Nhâm (V)　　Tân Chhin 陳親　Trần Thân (V)
Sim Liang 沈亮　Thẩm Lượng (V)　　Teng Kim 鄭金　Trịnh Kim (V)

CANTONESE NAMES

Can4 Fai1 Gwong1 陳輝光　Trần　　Can4 Zan3 Gei3 陳振記
　Huy Quang (V)　　　　　　　　Trần Chấn Ký
Can4 Jyu4 Sam1 陳如琛　Trần Như　Ho4 Ji4 Hing1 何宜興
　Thâm (V)　　　　　　　　　　Hà Nghi Hưng

NOTES

INTRODUCTION

1. *Đại Nam Thực Lục Chính Biên* 大南寔錄正編, part 2, 160:36. Hereafter *ĐNTL*.

2. The mother of the first emperor of the Nguyễn dynasty was named Lan, using the same character in Cai Tinglan's name (蘭). Following the custom of tabooing the names of royal family members, the character *lan* was replaced in official records with 香 (Ch. *xiang*; V. *hương*). Ngô and Poisson, *Nghiên Cứu Chữ Húy Việt Nam qua Các Triều Đại*, 124–28 and 326–27.

3. The two most comprehensive studies of Cai Tinglan's life are Cai Zhubin, *Cai Tinglan zhuan*; and Chen Yiyuan, *Cai Tinglan jiqi* Hainan zazhu.

4. In 1727, Penghu was defined as a subprefecture (*ting* 廳) of Fujian Province. For the history of Penghu, see Cai Zhubin, *Cai Tinglan zhuan*, 24–37.

5. Woodside, *Vietnam and the Chinese Model*, 174.

6. For a comprehensive survey of the civil examinations in late imperial China, see Elman, *A Cultural History of Civil Examinations in Late Imperial China*, especially 659.

7. Woodside, *Vietnam and the Chinese Model*, 171–72.

8. The Vietnamese did not hold formal school examinations for youth, so we have not provided the Vietnamese transliteration. Woodside, *Vietnam and the Chinese Model*, 176.

9. Elman, *A Cultural History of Civil Examinations in Late Imperial China*, 659; Cai Zhubin, *Cai Tinglan zhuan*, 40–41.

10. Wang Dezhao, "Qingdai de keju rushi yu zhengfu," 6. For provincial examinations in Fujian and the examinees from Taiwan, see Ding Xingyuan, "Mingdai Fujian xiangshi luodizhe de chulu jiqi yingxiang," 28–33; Liu Haifeng, "Taiwan juren zai Fujian xiangshi zhong de biaoxian," 68–77; Dai Xianqun, "Qingdai Fujian xiangshi yu Taiwan juren," 37–42.

11. Cai Zhubin, *Cai Tinglan zhuan*, 52.

12. For the shipwreck and Cai's adventure in Vietnam, see Chen Yiyuan, *Cai Tinglan jiqi* Hainan zazhu, 57–62; Huang Meiling, "Yiliao zhi wai de *yiyu* zhi lü";

Li Shuhui, "Lüyou, jiyi yu lunshu"; Tang Xiyong, "Chuannan yu haiwai lixian jingyan."

13. In fact, there were several shipwreck cases on this route recorded during the Qing dynasty. See Tang, "Chuannan yu haiwai lixian jingyan," 467–80. For the records of hurricanes and storms of the Penghu region, see Li Zhijun, *Fengxia zhi hai*.

14. *ĐNTL* II, 121:13.

15. *ĐNTL* II, 143:2.

16. *ĐNTL* II, 166:22.

17. *ĐNTL* II, 170:13.

18. *ĐNTL* II, 13:9.

19. *ĐNTL* II, 71:18. It was precedent to provide funds to merchants stranded in Vietnam. For example, in 1833, Minh Mạng ordered that a ship of Cantonese merchants who drifted to Quảng Nam be given three hundred strings of cash and three hundred *fang* of rice. *ĐNTL* II, 88:3.

20. You Jianshe 尤建設, "17 shiji houqi," 19.

21. Kuang Lu's 1634 *Chiya* was the first literati account of Guangxi. Miles, "Strange Encounters on the Cantonese Frontier."

22. For surveys on the editions of *Hainan zazhu* and how they were produced, see Chen Yiyuan, *Cai Tinglan jiqi* Hainan zazhu, 73–84; Yu Xiangdong, "Hainan zazhu de zuozhe yu banben," 93–96; Lin Jiahui, "Cai Tinglan *Hainan zazhu* yanjiu," 2–6. For a brief Vietnamese overview of Cai Tinglan's life, the publication history of the book, and its significance, see Vu Hướng Đông and Đinh Văn Minh, "Vài nét về tác giả và văn bản Hải Nam tạp trứ."

23. The National Library of China holds a first printing of the first edition, under call number 地 983.83/864; it holds a first printing of the second edition under the call number 地 983.83/864.1. The National Library in Taipei has only an incomplete copy of the second run of the second edition.

24. The above information is drawn from Chen Yiyuan, *Cai Tinglan jiqi* Hainan zazhu, 73–87. His authoritative study can be consulted for more detailed information about textual history, including the specific changes between editions. The French translation can be found in Leroux, *Recueil d'itinéraires et de voyages dans l'Asie Centrale et l'Extrême Orient*.

25. Cai Tinglan and Xia Deyi, *Hainan zazhu* 海南雜著.

26. Gotō Hitoshi, "Sai Teiran *Kainan zaccho* to sono shiyaku."

27. https://ctext.org/wiki.pl?if=gb&res=107349. Also see the digital version of Cai Tinglan and Xia Deyi, *Hainan zazhu* 海南雜著 at http://tcss.ith.sinica.edu.tw

/cgi-bin/gs32/gsweb.cgi/ccd=OIi5ab/ebookviewer?dbid=EB0000000042
&db=ebook.

28. Chen Lunjiong, *Haiguo wenjian lu*, 31.

29. White, *History of a Voyage to the China Sea*, 95–96.

30. Cooke, Li, and Anderson, *Tongking Gulf through History*.

31. Wheeler, "Placing the 'Chinese Pirates' of the Gulf of Tongking at the End of the Eighteenth Century."

32. Po, *The Blue Frontier*, 17.

33. Translated and quoted by Po, 64.

34. The classic comparison of Qing and Nguyễn governments is Woodside, *Vietnam and the Chinese Model*.

35. Taylor, *History of the Vietnamese*, 403.

36. See also Zhu Yunying, *Zhongguo wenhua dui Ri Han Yue de yingxiang*, 546–47.

37. Wheeler, "An Offshore Perspective on Vietnamese Zen," 145.

38. Wheeler, "Interests, Institutions, and Identity." Wang Gungwu's study shows the ways in which Chinese overseas, including the Minh Hương in Vietnam and the Peranakan or Straits Chinese, adopted local customs, adapted their own customs to fit in, intermarried, and entered government office, all while maintaining a sense of separate identity. Wang Gungwu, *The Chinese Overseas*, 80–82. For a pioneering study on the topic of overseas Chinese in Vietnam, see Fujiwara Riichirō, *Tōnan ajiashi no kenkyū*, 191–282. Also see You Jianshe, "17 shiji houqi"; and Qiu Puyan, "Yuenan Huaqiao shehui de xingcheng yu fazhan," 82–87.

39. Reid, "Chinese Trade and Southeast Asian Economic Expansion," 23.

40. Cooke and Li, *Water Frontier*, 3–6

41. Zhu Yunying, *Zhongguo wenhua dui Ri Han Yue de yingxiang*, 548.

42. For a discussion of the term *sojourn* in migration studies, see Wang Gungwu, "Sojourning."

43. Zhu Yunying, *Zhongguo wenhua dui Ri Han Yue de yingxiang*, 549.

44. Qiu Puyan, "Yuenan Huaqiao shehui de xingcheng yu fazhan," 82–83, 85. Also see Teng Lanhua and He Zhe, "*Yuenan youli ji* zhong suojian de Yuenan Beiqi Huaqiao Huaren tanxi." 62–68. Initially, Gia Long wanted the Minh Hương to join the *bang*, but they successfully resisted, arguing that their Vietnamese matrilineage set them apart from more recent arrivals. Wheeler, "Identity," 157.

45. For example, Hakka does not indicate any particular region but rather designates a language group or ethnicity. In another case, Fuzhou should be

part of Fujian Province in Qing China, but it was separated probably because the distinctive Fuzhou dialect of Hokkien was spoken there.

46. Wheeler, "Identity," 157.

47. Kuhn, *Chinese among Others*, 44.

48. For the text of the inscription in the temple, see Trịnh, Nguyễn, and Papin, *Tổng Tập Thác Bản Văn Khắc Hán Nôm*, 280.

49. Wheeler, "Interests, Institutions, and Identity," 157. For a Nguyễn prohibition on Qing merchants bringing Vietnamese women back with them to China as wives, see *Đại Nam Thực Lục Chính Biên II, juan* 62, 2.

50. Kuhn, *Chinese among Others*, 12.

51. Macauley, *Distant Shores*, 9.

52. Macauley, *Distant Shores*, 74.

53. Pomeranz. *The Great Divergence*.

54. Macauley, *Distant Shores*, 11–12. For the role of Chinese settlers in developing the Saigon region, see Choi Byung Wook, *Southern Vietnam under the Reign of Minh Mạng*, especially 38–39.

55. Chin, "The Junk Trade between South China and Nguyen Vietnam, 53–54, 63. Choi Byung Wook suggests that Vietnamese traders were less visible to Western visitors, contributing to their assumption that the Chinese dominated trade. *South China under the Reign of Minh Mạng*, 74–75.

56. Wang Gungwu, "Merchants without Empire." The Nguyễn did struggle to control the illegal export of rice, tax evasion by traders, and the smuggling of drugs. See Choi, *South China*, 74–81.

57. Xing Hang, "The Evolution of Maritime Chinese Historiography in the United States."

58. Miles, *Upriver Journeys*, 8–15.

59. Po, *The Blue Frontier*, 7.

60. Macauley, *Distant Shores*, ix.

61. Woodside, *Vietnam and the Chinese Model*, preface, np. For a study of one nineteenth-century Vietnamese scholar's intellectual engagement with the Confucian commonwealth, see Baldanza, "Books without Borders."

62. For "Sinophographic cosmopolis," see King, "Ditching 'Diglossia'"; page 6 has a discussion of various terms and their rationales. For "Sanskrit Cosmopolis," see Pollack, *The Language of the Gods in the World of Men*.

63. For James Matisoff's division of the origins of elite cultural influence in the Southeast between the Sinosphere and the Indosphere, see "Sino-Tibetan Linguistics: Present State and Future Prospects," 469–504. The term *Sinograph* was coined by Zev Handel. See his *Sinograph*, 10–11.

64. Millward, "We Need a New Approach to Teaching Chinese History."

65. Choi Byung Wook, "The Nguyen Dynasty's Policy toward Chinese," 93–95.

66. Vũ Đường Luân and Li Tana, "Chinese Merchants and Mariners in Nineteenth-Century Tongking," 150.

67. Zhongguo Shehui Kexueyuan Yuyan Yanjiusuo, Zhongguo Shehui Kexueyuan Minzuxue Yu Renleixue Yanjiusuo, and Xianggang Chengshi Daxue Yuyan Zixunkexue Yanjiu Zhongxin , Zhongguo yuyan ditu ji juan, map B1–15, B2–6; 111; Fujiansheng difangzhi bianzuan weiyuanhui, Fujiansheng zhi, 98–99. For the relationship between Min dialects and their adjacent dialects, see Ding Bangxin and Zhang Shuangqing, Minyu yanjiu jiqi yu zhoubian fangyan de guanxi. For the history of Hokkien and the Min dialect in general, see Norman, "The Mǐn Dialects in Historical Perspective"; Du Jialun, Minyu lishi cengci fenxi yu xiangguan yinbian.

68. Zhongguo yuyan ditu ji, Map B1–15; B1–18. For a comprehensive list of people whom Cai encountered, see Dai Kelai and Yu Xiangdong, "Cai Tinglan."

69. Simmons, "Whence Came Mandarin?," especially 72; Zhang Weidong, "Shilun jindai nanfang Guanhua de xingcheng jiqi diwei," 73–78.

70. It is unclear whether Cai asked Sim about what happened or if it was just Cai's assumption. Theoretically, there were many reasons that Sim might not have been able to interpret. For example, they might have been speaking a specific dialect that Sim could not understand. Alternatively, they could simply have told him that they preferred to have a written conversation with Cai through literary Chinese, since that was a common mode of communication among the literati in East Asia. In this way, they could also verify his identity as a Qing government–sponsored student. Note that this verification of his identity happened later during his trip.

71. For languages in early China, particularly Old Chinese, see Baxter, A Handbook of Old Chinese Phonology, 1–5; and Pulleyblank, Outline of Classical Chinese Grammar, 1–2.

72. See Gao Mingshi, "Bingong ke de qiyuan yu fazhan"; Wu Zongguo, Tangdai keju zhidu yanjiu, 25–35, 149–54; Miyazaki Ichisada, Kakyo, 1–18.

73. See, for example, Baldanza, Ming China and Vietnam, 179–98; Ge Zhaoguang, Xiangxiang yiyu, and Zhai zi Zhongguo, 157–65; Pore, "The Inquiring Literatus."

74. Brush talks were so natural for Vietnamese officials that they also attempted to communicate with Western visitors in written Latin. The American crew of John White's ship that visited Vietnam in 1823 called up their schoolboy

Latin to communicate with two mandarins who had learned it from French missionaries. White, *History of a Voyage*, 79.

75. For the linguistic situation of Vietnam, see DeFrancis, *Colonialism and Language Policy in Viet Nam*. For a description of the Nôm script, see pages 24–26.

76. See Ngô Đức Thọ and Hoàng Văn Lâ's Vietnamese translation for a more comprehensive accounting of such mistakes: Trần Ích Nguyên (陳益源), *Thái Đình Lan & tác phẩm Hải Nam Tạp Trứ.*

77. Alistair Lamb, *Mandarin Road to Old Hué.*

78. Chin, "The Junk Trade," 61.

79. Lamb, 33; White, 65.

80. See Choi Byung Wook, *South China under the Reign of Minh Mạng*, 87–88.

81. For a more comprehensive description of the clothing of Nguyễn officials, see Trần Quang Đức, *Ngàn Năm Áo Mũ*, 297–334.

82. Cai may have misheard *bản thổ công* 本土公, "local deity." The eighteenth-century Catholic priest Adriano di St. Thecla described the worship of Thổ Công, five brothers who were deified for killing a problem tiger. Di St. Thecla, *Opusculum de Sectis apud Sinenses et Tunkinses*, 147.

83. Wickberg, *The Chinese in Philippine Life*, 193–94.

84. Li, "Between Mountains and the Sea," 71–72.

85. Li, "Between Mountains and the Sea," 73.

86. Dutton, *The Tay Son Uprising*, 45; Choi Byung Wook, *Southern Vietnam under the Reign of Minh Mạng*.

87. Wheeler, "Placing the 'Chinese Pirates,'" 51. Following the Vietnamese historical record, Wheeler refers to He Xianwen as He Xiwen in his article. See also Murray, *Pirates of the South China Coast*.

88. Woodside, *Vietnam and the Chinese Model*, 298n22; Kelley, *Beyond the Bronze Pillars*, 79n26.

89. Kelley, *Bronze Pillars*, 78–9. See also Choi Byung Wook, *Southern Vietnam*, 45n1.

90. For an interpretation of the economic and political underpinnings of the Nông Văn Vân rebellion, see Vũ Đường Luân, "The Politics of Frontier Mining." See also Davis, *Imperial Bandits*, 16, 18, 30.

91. For the use of *hainan* as *nanhai*, see *Fujian tongzhi* 福建通志 (Taipei: Taiwan Yinhang jingji yanjiushi, 1960), 239 and 822. It is true that *hainan* could be used to indicate Vietnam as in the eleventh-century text by Zhao Rushi 趙汝適, *Zhufan zhi* 諸蕃志 (Taipei: Taiwan Yinhang jingji yanjiushi, 1961), 57. However,

in the text, Cai also hints that the name is related to *nanhai*. Moreover, the first chapter does not record his travel in Vietnam, but only his journey on the South Seas. Therefore, "South Seas" captures the multiple connotations better.

92. Li, "Between Mountains and the Sea," and personal communication, July 3, 2019. Ngô Đức Thọ's Vietnamese translation also transliterates this word as *phở*.

93. Vũ Đường Luân, "The Politics of Frontier Mining," 38.

94. We are grateful to Dr. Vũ for sharing these citations, personal communication, February 23, 2021.

95. Choi Byung Wook, "The Nguyen Dynasty's Policy toward Chinese," 90.

96. Taylor, *History of the Vietnamese*, 1–5.

97. Roberts, *Embassy to the Eastern Courts of Cochin-China, Siam, and Muscat,* 182.

ZHOU'S FOREWORD

1. *Đại Nam Thực Lục Chính Biên* 大南寔錄正編, part 2, 160:36.

LIU'S FOREWORD

1. Su Shi 蘇軾, *Su Shi shiji* 蘇軾詩集 (Beijing: Zhonghua, 1982), 43:2366.

2. During the Qing dynasty, Qiongzhou was under the jurisdiction of Guangdong Province.

SECOND DEDICATION

1. Bai Juyi was a Tang poet (772–846) whose fame reached even Silla (57 BCE–935 CE), a kingdom located on the Korean peninsula.

RECORD OF PERIL ON THE HIGH SEAS

1. One watch is two hours and twenty-four minutes long.

2. See the introduction for a discussion of these places.

3. The goddess Mazu protected sailors and maritime enterprises and was especially popular along the southeast coast of China and in Chinese diasporic communities across Southeast Asia.

4. A *li* is approximately a third of a mile. From the Tang dynasty to 1929, one

li was defined as 1,800 *bu* 步, which was 1,800 *chi*. Since in Qing China, one *chi* was often equal to 0.32 meter, one *li* could be 576 meters.

5. This term remains a common label for Chinese in Canton, Hokkien, and Teochew.

6. The name in the original is 占畢羅嶼, which indicates the modern day Chàm islands (Cù lao Chàm).

7. This is one of a small number of lines that changed between the first and second editions. We chose to translate this line from the first edition: 而以詩自鳴於海外之國. In the revised line, 因以擴見聞於海外之國, the emphasis changed from earning fame through poetry composition to enlarging one's knowledge of a foreign country.

TRAVELOGUE OF THE FIERY WASTELAND

1. For an 1823 description of Vietnamese official garb by a lieutenant in the US Navy, see White, *History of a Voyage to the China Sea*, 37. He describes officials wearing wooden sandals and wide black trousers with a red silk sash, with black crepe turbans. A similar description was made by Thomas Wade in 1855, in Lamb, *Mandarin Road to Old Hué*, 317; and in Roberts, *Embassy to the Eastern Courts*, 181.

2. Now called Sa Cần station, at the mouth of the Trà Bồng River in Quảng Ngãi Province. Ngô and Hoàng, *Thái Đình Lan*, 171n16.

3. The British army officer Charles Chapman similarly writes that Vietnamese rowers sang "a song not destitute of harmony" during a trip upriver to Hội An in 1778. Anthologized in Lamb, *Mandarin Road to Old Hue*, 105. John White writes that Vietnamese rowers who approach his ship are "cheered by a measured and monotonous recitative" but later finds out that they are in fact jeering "mot quan," or one string of cash, their paltry monthly salary allotted by the government; *History of a Voyage*, 60 and 212.

4. Here, in referring to "prefectural governor," Cai used the phrase *futangguan* 府堂官. He is speaking generally of leading officials in the prefecture. Later in this text, Cai used the same phrase to refer to two different official titles, namely, provincial magistrate and the officials of Imperial Household Department, or *neiwufu* 內務府.

5. "Vạn" denotes a river market. In the original, Cai Tinglan was using Han characters to transcribe what he heard. We are following Li Tana's transcription. Ngô Đức Thọ and Hoàng Văn Lâu's 2009 translation transcribes it instead as Đò Ván.

6. China followed the same naming practice, so it is not clear why Cai Tinglan is specially calling attention to it.

7. According to Ngô Đức Thọ, this place name is in error. Perhaps Cai Tinglan heard Chính Mông, the name of the hamlet that contained Quảng Ngãi city, and mis-transcribed it. Cù Mông is the name of a mountain range south of Cai's route (Ngô and Hoàng, *Thái Đình Lan*, 176n29). The place he is in is Quảng Ngãi city.

8. Here we translate the lines in the Sino-Nom Institute's copy (HVv.80). Later editions changed these lines to say, "I followed them into the city, and gawkers lined the street."

9. This version is from HVv.80. Later editions say, "They both rose and leaned forward with folded hands in response to my bow."

10. For Fujian Association, or Fujian bang 福建幫, Philip A. Kuhn's definition: "'Bang' (gang, or sojourner association) is an organized, hierarchical urban group based on dialect, devoted to promoting the business interests of its members and protecting its economic turf from rival dialect groups. It is typically headed by a prominent and wealthy man"; *Chinese among Others*, 54n67.

11. Cai Tinglan, following Chinese practice, refers to the Vietnamese ruler as a king (*wang/vương* 王). Vietnamese sources use the term emperor.

12. The four core texts of the Confucian canon and basis of the civil service examinations: the *Analects*, the *Mencius*, the *Doctrine of the Mean*, and the *Great Learning*.

13. Here Cai Tinglan is using a Chinese character to transcribe the sound of *thầy*, a polite term of address for men. Here we are following Ngô and Hoàng, *Thái Đình Lan*, 180n38.

14. Woodside writes that teachers trace characters on boards covered with soil or clay, and their pupils would then trace the characters themselves. Woodside, *Vietnam and the Chinese Model*, 188

15. "Vạn" suggests a river market comprised of house boats. Many of these traders would have been Chinese traders involved in the transshipment of forest products. See Phú Bình, "Tứ Bàn từ 'man' đến 'chợ.'"

16. Cai used the word *xunfu guan* 巡撫官 to refer to the relevant officials in Vietnam instead of the more commonly used word *xunfu* 巡撫 for the official in charge of a province. Therefore, we translate *xunfu guan* as "provincial governor" and use "governor" to refer to the *xunfu* position in the Qing dynasty.

17. Phan Thanh Giản (1796–1867) became a palace graduate in 1826 and traveled to China as an envoy in 1832. A southerner descended from Minh hương families from Fujian on both sides, Phan Thanh Giản went on to have important

positions in the Nguyễn government, including governor of Nam Ngãi, soon after meeting Cai Tinglan. He is most remembered today for negotiating the Treaty of Saigon with France in 1862, traveling to France in 1863, and dying by suicide after France invaded the southern territories, then under his governorship, in 1867. See Ngô Đức Thọ et al, *Các Nhà Khoa Bảng Việt Nam*, 653.

18. This is an alternate name for Ngũ Hành Sơn, or the Marble Mountains. We are grateful to Drs. Le Thi Mai and Li Tana for verifying this.

19. There must be a corruption in the text here because two feet is not the right unit of measurement for a mountain.

20. 1 *chi* = 32 cm in Qing China.

21. Hải Sơn Quản 海山關. The name is now Ocean Cloud Pass (Đèo Hải Vân).

22. *Xingxing* 猩猩.

23. *Wei* is an approximate measure word for the perimeter of objects. It usually stands for the perimeter of a circle as big as the length of ones' arm span or as small as that from one's thumb to the index finger of the same hand. In this case, it seems to refer to the latter length.

24. The stream he is referring to is the Perfume River. Cai tends to use the word *xi* 溪, meaning stream or creek, when he does not record the proper name of the river. He probably uses "stream" here for that reason and not because it appears small.

25. For a similar description of Huế, circa 1778, see the account of Charles Chapman, anthologized by Alistair Lamb in *Mandarin Road to Old Hue*, 109. Chapman visited during the Tây Sơn period, and the city walls were repaired well before Cai Tinglan arrived decades later. John Crawfurd's account from 1822 describes the city's defenses as "truly extraordinary" and claims that most of their artillery was cast in Cochinchina; *Mandarin Road*, 246.

26. The second edition changed "I wrote a congratulatory essay" to "I brought my name card" 攜名版. Here the "prefectural governor" or *futangguan* refers to the prefect of Thừa Thiên.

27. The revised edition substitutes "and my friends questioned me closely" 交致研詰 instead of "met with praise."

28. *Sheji tan* 社稷壇. This is an altar where the emperor would make sacrifices to benefit the state.

29. 午門 Wumen (Ch.), Ngọ Môn (V.). Woodside calls it the "Zenith Gate," *Vietnam and the Chinese Model*, 128. There are four main gates; this is the southern gate.

30. *Hongyi pao* 紅衣炮. This refers to a muzzle-loading style cannon first introduced by the Dutch and English and then produced in improved form in China. *Red* refers to Dutch, nicknamed "red-haired barbarians" in Chinese. Originally, this style of cannon was called *hồng di pháo* 紅夷炮, "red barbarian cannon," but red coat cannon came into common use during the Qing because Manchus objected to the term *barbarian*. See Andrade, *The Gunpowder Age*, 197–201.

31. Literally, the text says that he was a tributary student, indicating that he studied at the Quốc tử giám or Imperial College, located in Huế during the Nguyễn dynasty.

32. Here Cai Tinglan uses a character in the Vietnamese demotic script chữ Nôm for chợ, *market* (㕵), suggesting that someone wrote down the name for him. Immediately below, for Chợ Ròn 㕵市, he uses the Chinese character for market and a Nôm word to transcribe Ròn. It seems likely that Cai did not understand how the Nôm script was used in Vietnam.

33. Present-day Đèo Ngang, at the border of Quảng Bình and Hà Tĩnh Provinces.

34. Present-day Kỳ Anh County in Hà Tĩnh.

35. Present-day Vĩnh.

36. *Fanjiang* 番薑.

37. Here Cai is using Holland to mean from overseas or from Western traders more generally.

38. Cai Tinglan may have misunderstood this. The governor-general of that time was not surnamed Nguyễn or related to the royal family.

39. As noted by James M. Hargett, this bird is a member of the pheasant family and is sometimes called peacock-pheasant. They existed in great numbers in neighboring Guangxi in the twelfth century but can no longer be found. Fan Chengda, Hargett, *Treatises of the Supervisor of the Cinnamon Sea*, 60n3.

40. Although there is a famous Nguyễn official named Ông Ích Khiêm (1829–1884), he would have been a child at this time. The identical name must be a coincidence or a mistake.

41. Present-day Phủ Lý in Hà Nam.

42. Here *futang guan* is used as another way to refer to provincial magistrate, instead of prefectural governor as previously mentioned.

43. This distance appears to be in error.

44. We use Jyutping to transcribe Cantonese pronunciations. For the tones, see glossary.

45. The Red River (sông Hồng).

46. The rebellion of the Trưng sisters (Hai Bà Trưng) against Han dynasty rule from 40 to 43 CE remains one of the most celebrated events in Vietnamese history. The earliest extant source about the rebellion is the *Hou Han Shu* (History of the Later Han 後漢書), which records that the Han general Ma Han had the sisters beheaded. The temple Cai Tinglan visited was commissioned by Lý Anh Tông in the twelfth century after the Trưng sisters appeared to him in a dream as rain spirits.

47. It is not clear what places Cai Tinglan is referring to here.

48. A mountain pass in the southern part of Lạng Sơn Province. Vietnamese: Quỷ Môn Quan.

49. 薏苡 or *ý dĩ*. Also commonly known as coix seeds. Used as both a food and medicine.

50. *Yin* and *yang*, or heaven and earth.

51. Legend has it that Ma Yuan erected two bronze pillars to mark the southern border of the Han empire after he conquered Giao Chỉ (northern Vietnam). Although no trace of them has ever been found, the story and purported location were repeated throughout the imperial period.

52. It is not clear who Cai Tinglan means by "the governor of Bianzhou," and it is probably a mistake. He most likely is referring to the ultimately unsuccessful 1788–89 Qing invasion of northern Vietnam to depose the Tây Sơn dynasty (1778–1802) and restore the Lê dynasty.

53. This refers to the uprising of Nông Văn Vân, a local *tusi*/thổ ty who rebelled when the Nguyễn state attempted to remove him from his position, resulting in fighting between 1833–35.

54. Ngô Thì Nhậm (1746–1803) was a prominent scholar-official of the Tây Sơn who earned his Presented Scholar degree in 1775. His father Ngô Thì Sĩ (1725–80), an important historian, was governor of Lạng Sơn in 1780. It is possible that Cai Tinglan is mixing up father and son. In fact, Ngô Thì Ngậm developed the cave system and had temples dedicated to the three religions, Buddhism, Daoism, and Confucianism.

55. Lê Hữu Dung (1745–?) passed the examination as palace graduate in 1775 and served as an envoy to the Qing dynasty. See Ngô Đức Thọ et al, *Các Nhà Khoa Bảng Việt Nam*, 630.

56. Tam Thanh, or Sanqing 三清, is a Daoist concept originally indicating the three heavenly realms, Yuqing 玉清 (Jade Clarity), Shangqing 上清 (Highest Clarity), and Taiqing 太清 (Great Clarity). Later it indicates the three deities from the three realms, respectively: Celestial Worthy of Original Commence-

ment (Yuanshi tianzun 元始天尊), the Celestial Worthy of Numinous Treasure (Lingbao tianzun 靈寶天尊), and the Celestial Worthy of the Way and Its Virtue (Daode tianzun 道德天尊). See the entry "Sanqing 三清" written by Livia Kohn in Pregadio, *The Encyclopedia of Taoism*, 840–44.

57. "Water without roots" (*wugen shui* 無根水) refers to water that is not from the ground, such as rain drops or dew.

58. Su Ruolan, also known as Su Hui, was a fourth-century CE poet. Cai Tinglan likely thinks this is ridiculous because Su Ruolan was known to have lived in Shaanxi and Gansu, nowhere near Vietnam. Dou Tao was her husband. As early as the fifteenth century, this story was localized in Vietnam. For an explanation, see Hieu M. Phung, "Land & Water," 54–56. For a discussion of Awaiting Husband Boulders in neighboring Guangxi, associated by Kuang Lu with Chinese merchants married to native women in Guangxi, see Miles, "Strange Encounters," 142–45.

59. Nhị Thanh (二青, literally, "two green") and Tam Thanh (三青, "three green") are named such because of natural markings on the cave walls that looked like those characters. They remain popular sightseeing destinations in Lạng Sơn and can be found in English language guidebooks as Nhi Thanh and Tam Thanh Grottoes. It is unclear what cave Đại Thanh (大青 "big green") refers to.

60. In the first edition, this is 310 *li*.

61. The Jianwen emperor was the second emperor of the Ming dynasty (r. 1398–1402). One of his uncles rebelled and ascended the Ming throne as the Yongle emperor. Although the Yongle emperor maintained that the Jianwen emperor had died in a fire and presented his body, rumors persisted that the former emperor was living in hiding in the South as a monk.

62. Xiangshan Island, renamed Zhongshan Island in the twentieth century.

63. Anqi Sheng was a legendary immortal who lived in the sea, mentioned in several early Chinese texts.

64. Meaning that in Huizhou, the clouds block the view of the peak, while farther away in Guangzhou, only the peak is visible.

65. The mausoleum of the famous Song dynasty poet and statesman Su Shi's (1037–1101) concubine Wang Zhaoyun.

66. While certain terms such as horizon (*diping* 地平) and procedures point to the armillary sphere technique introduced by Johann Adam Schall von Bell (1591–1666) and others, it is unclear what the other terms Cai uses refer to. For more information on this technique, see Zhang Baichun, "The Introduction of European Astronomical Instruments."

67. Zhao Shenzhen received the palace graduate title in 1796 and died in 1822.

He served as governor-general of Zhejiang and Fujian and had a particular interest in promoting worthy scholars.

68. Round communal houses found only in Fujian Province, unique to the Hakka.

69. Zhu Xi (1130–1200), a neo-Confucian scholar born in Fujian Province.

70. The name Yangzhi 仰止 is from the line in "Che xia" 車舝 of the *Book of Poetry* (*Shijing* 詩經): "Behold a high mountain with awe" 高山仰止. This line was famously used by Sima Qian 司馬遷 (145–? BCE) to praise the virtue of Confucius. See Sima Qian, *Shiji*, 47:1947.

VIETNAM CHRONICLE

1. A watch is two hours and twenty-four minutes, so approximately two hundred hours or eight days.

2. Tây Kinh, literally "western capital," was the name used by the Hồ dynasty for their capital in Thanh Hóa. However, Cai Tinglan is mistakenly placing it in Quảng Nam. Đông Kinh is a historical name for Hà Nội, literally "eastern capital," which is usually written in Western languages as Tonkin or Tongking. Although this term refers to a city, it is also used to designate the larger region.

3. Legendary emperors from the third millennium BCE.

4. In this paragraph, Cai Tinglan is listing the Đinh dynasty (968–80), the Early Lê dynasty (980–1009), the Lý dynasty (1009–1225), and the Trần dynasty (1225–1400) by founding emperor. The Yuan dynasty attacked Trần-era Vietnam three times, but each campaign ended in failure. Cai Tinglan miswrote the final name: Trần Quang Nhuế 陳光昺 should be Trần Hoảng 陳晃.

5. More commonly known as Hồ Hán Thương.

6. More commonly known as Lê Huyền Tông.

7. We have corrected the text here. He wrote 阮光年 rather than 阮光平, an alternate name of Nguyễn Huệ.

8. The above historical overview uses the names used in Chinese historical records rather than Vietnamese records and is generally written from a Chinese perspective. It seems more likely that Cai derived his understanding here from Chinese texts than from conversation with Vietnamese people.

9. This is Nguyễn Phúc Ánh (1762–1820), who took the reign name Gia Long after establishing the Nguyễn dynasty in 1802.

10. Historical names for Sài Gòn, now Hồ Chí Minh City. Cai Tinglan is transcribing what he heard or what he was shown. Lũng Nại is more recognizable in Vietnamese as "Đồng Nai 鹿野" (Donnai) but does seem to reflect a con-

temporary pronunciation. George Staunton, secretary to the Lord Macartney mission to China of 1793, refers to "the province of Donai, or southern part of Cochin-china," in his account, 376. See also the 1822 journal of John Crawfurd, head of British mission to Siam and Cochinchina: "Two American ships have obtained full cargoes at the Port of Saigon, or Longnai, as it is called by the Chinese." Crawfurd, *Journal*, 44. For the history of the place-name Đồng Nai, see Choi Byung Wook, *Southern Vietnam under the Reign of Minh Mạng*, 23.

11. Thái Đức is the reign name of Nguyễn Nhạc (r. 1778–1888), one of the founding brothers of the Tây Sơn dynasty (1778–1802). We have corrected where the text reverses the order of the characters as Định Bình. This is referring not to the current province but to the port city now known as Quy Nhơn that is the capital of the province.

12. Nguyễn Huệ, one of the Tây Sơn brothers, who reigned as the Quang Trung emperor from 1788 to 1792.

13. In fact, Thái Đức (the reign name of Nguyễn Nhạc), Quang Trung (the reign name of Nguyễn Huệ), and Nguyễn Lữ, the founders of the Tây Sơn, were biological brothers. There is no textual evidence that they became blood brothers with Nguyễn Ánh, the future Gia Long emperor.

14. Cai Tinglan slightly misunderstands the political situation, but in a way that is revealing of how people thought at the time. See introduction.

15. The junior mentor Trần Quang Diệu and the grand minister of the masses Vũ Văn Dũng were two of the most important Tây Sơn generals. Both were captured (see below) and beheaded in Huế in 1802.

16. The events that Cai Tinglan is describing, the siege of the citadel of Quy Nhơn, occurred in 1800–1. The son-in-law was actually Gia Long's brother-in-law (married to his sister), Võ Tánh. Võ Tánh in fact blew himself up with gunpowder as part of negotiations for the Tây Sơn to spare his soldiers.

17. He Xianwen or Hà Hiến Văn 何獻文. This person is mostly likely He Xiwen (Hà Hý Văn 何喜文), actually a native of Sichuan, who was active in Fujian and Guangdong before arriving in Vietnam.

18. In fact, Quang Trung had died in 1792. Cai Tinglan is most likely mixing him up with his son, Nguyễn Quang Toản.

19. Đông Kinh and Thăng Long are two historical names of the city now called Hà Nội. Thăng Long is also written with the characters 昇龍, "Ascending Dragon."

20. This refers to the Lê Văn Khôi revolt, 1833–1835.

21. The Nông Văn Vân 農文雲 rebellion, 1833–35. Incidentally, Nông Văn Vân was Lê Văn Khôi's brother-in-law.

22. The second edition changed this line to "The people I spoke with about this all blamed Tang people."

23. The Quang Trung emperor's son Nguyễn Quang Toản reigned from 1792 until his execution in 1802. His two reign names were Cảnh Thịnh and Bảo Hưng. In the text, the character *hưng* 興 is mistakenly written as *điển* 典. Cai Tinglan also mistakenly thinks these names describe two different people. He is also probably mixing up Nguyễn Quang Toản with his father. The Quang Trung emperor did not lead a gang from the mountains, having died in 1792 at the height of Tây Sơn power. His son did have to flee before the Nguyễn army, although he also did not lead a gang in the mountains.

24. Meaning government control cannot reach faraway places.

25. This refers to the fact that unlike the Qing dynasty, the palace examinations in Nguyễn Vietnam did not grant the special titles for the top three winners. See the introduction for the contemporary situation in Qing China.

26. John White described these contraptions thusly while in Saigon in December 1819: "There are no wheel-carriages in Cochin China, either for pleasure or utility. Persons of distinction are carried in hammocks of cotton netting, generally blue, in which is a mattress and pillows to recline upon. The hammock is suspended to a pole, over which is placed a canopy resembling a huge tortoise-shell, and made impervious to the weather by a glossy black varnish; the vehicle is carried by four or six men, one half at each end." White, *History of a Voyage*, 319.

27. For a longer description and illustrations of soldiers' uniforms, see Trần Quang Đức, *Ngàn Năm Áo Mũ*, 345–47.

28. Later editions insert this line: "They always use rattan switches for flogging. For petty crimes people wear a bamboo cangue and for more serious crimes they wear a wooden cangue with handcuffs."

29. Here Cai Tinglan uses the Chinese characters *luanba* 亂霸 phonetically to represent the Vietnamese phrase "*nằm vạ.*"

30. Elephant and tiger battles were indeed staged for the royal family in an open field, as described in Cai. In 1830, the Hổ Quyền arena was built outside Huế, and hosted the fights until 1904.

31. The character for *chú* is 叔.

32. Here the text uses Jiutian Yuannü 九天元女 instead of the more common 九天玄女 Jiutian Xuannü.

33. Here Cai Tinglan is using Chinese characters to phonetically represent Vietnamese sounds, but it is not entirely clear what word he is writing. There is also variation between editions. The second edition has *bản khẩu*本扣.

34. The term used here, *luantong* 孌童, is often translated as catamite and implies sexual availability.

35. The term *tianmo wu* 天魔舞 literally means the "dance of the heavenly monsters," but here it has a Buddhist connotation.

36. This story comes from *The Romance of the Three Kingdoms* (*Sanguo yanyi*, fourteenth century).

37. The character Cai Tinglan uses is 喃喃, the same character, transcribed as Nôm, used to designate the Vietnamese demotic script. Cai, however, never mentions Nôm in his account, so his use of the character is probably coincidental.

38. For more on this shipbuilding technique, see Preston, "The Use of Basketry," 23–58.

39. By saying the "Western ships are terrified," the text refers to the woven ships in battle against the Dutch. See the relevant passage by the contemporary of Cai Tinglan, Xu Feng'en 許奉恩 (ca. 1862) in *Licheng*, 9:256.

40. Peanuts here are called first *luohuasheng* 落花生 and then *tudou* 土豆. Tudou usually means potato, but it was a variant for peanut in Taiwan.

41. Da Zhang walked across China from east to west and Shu Hai walked from north to south. This myth can be found in early Chinese texts such as *Shanhai jing* 山海經, *Huainanzi* 淮南子, and the *Wuyue Chunqiu* 吳越春秋.

POSTSCRIPT ONE

1. Liu Hong'ao 劉鴻翔 (1778–1849) was the surveillance commissioner of Taiwan in 1836, when this postscript was written.

2. Xiong put Cai among great authors in traditional China who experienced exile and died by drowning: Qu Yuan (?–278 BCE) was exiled twice, to Ankang of modern day Shaanxi Province, and Qingyang of modern day Anhui Province, respectively; Wang Bo (650–675 CE) visited his exiled father in Vietnam and died on the way back; Li Bai (701–762 CE) was sentenced to be exiled to Yelang in modern day Guizhou Province and was pardoned on his way there.

3. *Shizhou* 十洲, literally, "ten isles." This phrase evokes distant places filled with amazing things.

POSTSCRIPT TWO

1. The circuit intendant and the prefect refer to Zhou Kai and Liu Hong'ao, respectively. However, it is worth mentioning that in his preface, Liu was already promoted to surveillance commissioner of Shaanxi Province.

BIBLIOGRAPHY

Andrade, Tonio. *Gunpowder Age: China, Military Innovation, and the Rise of the West in World History.* Princeton, NJ: Princeton University Press, 2017.

Baldanza, Kathlene. "Books without Borders: Phạm Thận Duật (1825–1885) and the Culture of Knowledge in Mid-Nineteenth-Century Vietnam." *Journal of Asian Studies* 77, no. 3 (August 2018): 713–40.

——— . *Ming China and Vietnam: Negotiating Borders in Early Modern Asia.* Cambridge, UK: Cambridge University Press, 2016.

Baxter, William. *A Handbook of Old Chinese Phonology.* New York: De Gruyter Mouton, 1992.

Cai Tinglan 蔡廷蘭 and Xia Deyi 夏德儀, eds. *Hainan zazhu* 海南雜著. Taiwan wenxian congkan 台灣文獻叢刊. Taibei: Taiwan Yinhang Jingji Yanjiushi, 1959.

Cai Zhubin 蔡主賓. *Cai Tinglan zhuan* 蔡廷蘭傳. Jinmen: Jinmenxian Zhengfu Wenhua Ju, 2005.

Campbell, William. *A Dictionary of the Amoy Vernacular Spoken throughout the Prefectures of Chin-chiu, Chiang-chiu and Formosa.* Yokohama: Fukuin Print Co., 1913.

Chen Lunjiong 陳倫炯. *Haigui wenjian lu* 海國聞見錄. Taipei: Taiwan Yinhang Yanjiu Shi, 1958.

Chen Yiyuan 陳益源. *Cai Tinglan jiqi* Hainan zazhu 蔡廷蘭及其《海南雜著》. Taipei: Liren, 2006.

Chin, James Kong. "The Junk Trade between South China and Nguyen Vietnam in the Late Eighteenth and Early Nineteenth Centuries." In Cooke and Li, *Water Frontier,* 53–68.

Choi Byung Wook. "The Nguyen Dynasty's Policy toward Chinese on the Water Frontier in the First Half of the Nineteenth Century." In Cooke and Li, *Water Frontier,* 85–100.

——— . *Southern Vietnam under the Reign of Minh Mạng (1820–1841): Central Policies and Local Response.* Ithaca, NY: Cornell Southeast Asia Program Publications, 2004.

Cooke, Nola, and Tana Li, eds. *Water Frontier: Commerce and the Chinese in the Lower Mekong Region, 1750–1880.* Lanham, MD: Rowman & Littlefield, 2004.

Cooke, Nola, Tana Li, and James A. Anderson, eds. *The Tongking Gulf through History.* Philadelphia: University of Pennsylvania Press, 2011.

Crawfurd, John. *Journal of an Embassy from the Governor-General of India to the Courts of Siam and Cochin China.* Kuala Lumpur: Oxford University Press, 1967. First published 1830 by H. Holburn, London.

Dai Kelai [Đới Khả Lai] 戴可來. "Hoa Kiều và Người Hoa ở Việt Nam trong *Hải Nam tạp trước* của Thái Đình Lan." Việt Nam học—Kỷ yếu hội thảo quốc tế lần thứ nhất [Proceedings from the first international conference of Vietnamese studies] (1998): 315–33. https://repository.vnu.edu.vn/handle/VNU_123/20603.

Dai Kelai 戴可來 and Yu Xiangdong 于向東. "Cai Tinglan *Hainan zazhu* zhong suoji Yuenan Huaqiao Huaren 蔡廷蘭《海南雜著》中所記越南華僑華人." *Huaqiao Huaren lishi yanjiu*, no. 1 (1997).

Đại Nam Thực Lục Chính Biên 大南寔錄正編 [Veritable records of the great south, principal records]. Reprint, Tokyo: Institute of Cultural and Linguistic Studies, Keio University, 1961.

Dai Xianqun 戴顯群. "Qingdai Fujian xiangshi yu Taiwan juren 清代福建鄉試與台灣舉人." *Jiaoyu yu kaoshi*, no. 1 (2018).

Davis, Bradley Camp. *Imperial Bandits: Outlaws and Rebels in the China-Vietnam Borderlands.* Seattle: University of Washington Press, 2017.

DeFrancis, John. *Colonialism and Language Policy in Viet Nam.* New York: Mouton, 1977.

Di St. Thecla, Father Adriano. Olga Dror, translator and annotator, with collaboration of Mariya Berezovska in Latin translation. *Opusculum de Sectis apud Sinenses et Tunkinenses (A Small Treatise on the Sects among the Chinese and Tonkinese): A Study of Religion in China and North Vietnam in the Eighteenth Century.* Ithaca: Southeast Asia Program Publications, Cornell University, 2002.

Ding Bangxin 丁邦新 and Zhang Shuangqing 張雙慶, eds. *Minyu yanjiu jiqi yu zhoubian fangyan de guanxi* 閩語研究及其與周邊方言的關係. Hong Kong: Chinese University of Hong Kong Press, 2002.

Ding Xingyuan 丁星淵. "Mingdai Fujian xiangshi luodizhe de chulu jiqi yingxiang" 明代福建鄉試落第者的出路及其影響. *Haixia jiaoyu yanjiu*, no. 4 (2019).

Đỗ Văn Ninh. *Từ Điển Chức Quan Việt Nam* [Dictionary of Vietnamese official titles]. Hà Nội: Nhà Xuất Bản Thông Tấn, 2018.

Đới Khả Lai. "Hoa kiều và người Hoa ở Việt Nam trong" Hải Nam tạp trước"
của Thái Đình Lan." *Kỷ yếu Hội nghị* 1998: 315–33.

Du Jialun 杜佳倫. *Minyu lishi cengci fenxi yu xiangguan yinbian tantao* 閩語歷史
層次分析與相關音變探討. Shanghai: Zhongxi Shuju, 2014.

Dutton, George. *The Tay Son Uprising: Society and Rebellion in Eighteenth Century Vietnam.* Honolulu: University of Hawai'i Press, 2006.

Elman, Benjamin. *A Cultural History of Civil Examinations in Late Imperial
China.* Berkeley: University of California Press, 2000.

Fan Chengda, and James M. Hargett, trans. *Treatises of the Supervisor and
Guardian of the Cinnamon Sea: The Natural World and Material Culture of
12th Century South China.* Seattle: University of Washington Press, 2010.

Fujian tongzhi 福建通志. Taipei: Taiwan Yinhang jingji yanjiushi, 1960.

Fujiansheng difangzhi bianzuan weiyuanhui 福建省地方志編纂委員會 ed. *Fujiansheng zhi: Fangyan zhi* 福建省志：方言志. Beijing: Fangzhi, 1998.

Fujiwara Riichirō 藤原利一郎. *Tōnan ajiashi no kenkyū* 東南アジア史の研究.
Kyōto: Hōzōkan, 1986.

Gao Mingshi 高明士. "Bingong ke de qiyuan yu fazhan: Jianshu keju de qiyuan
yu Dongya shiren gongtong chushen zhi dao" 賓貢科的起源與發展——兼
述科舉的起源與東亞士人共同出身之道. *Tangshi luncun* 6 (1995): 68–109.

Ge Zhaoguang 葛兆光. *Xiangxiang yiyu: Du Lichao Chaoxian Hanwen Yanxing
wenxian zhaji* 想象異域——讀李朝朝鮮漢文燕行文獻札記. Beijing: Zhonghua, 2014.

———. *Zhai zi Zhongguo: Chongjian youguan "Zhongguo" de lishi lunshu* 宅茲
中國：重建有關「中國」的歷史論述. Beijing: Zhonghua, 2011.

Gotō Hitoshi 後藤均, ed. "Sai Teiran *Kainan zaccho* to sono shiyaku" 蔡廷蘭『
海南雜著』とその試訳, Kainan zaccho o yomukai 海南雜著を読む会, *Shien*
54, no. 1 (1993): 81–113.

Handel, Zev. *Sinography: The Borrowing and Adaptation of the Chinese Script.*
Leiden: Brill, 2019.

Hang, Xing. "The Evolution of Maritime Chinese Historiography in the
United States: Toward a Transnational and Interdisciplinary Approach."
Journal of Modern Chinese History 14, no. 1 (2020): 152–71.

Huang Meiling 黃美玲. "Yiliao zhi wai de *yiyu* zhi lü: Guan *Pihai jiyou* yu
Hainan zazhu de lüyou shiye 意料之外的「異域」之旅——觀《裨海紀
遊》與《海南雜著》的旅遊視野." *Gaoyi tongshi jiaoyu xuebao* no. 3 (2008):
151–72

Hucker, Charles O. *Dictionary of Official Titles in Imperial China.* Stanford, CA:
Stanford University Press, 1985.

King, Ross. "Ditching 'Diglossia': Describing Ecologies of the Spoken and Inscribed in Pre-modern Korea." *Sungkyun Journal of East Asian Studies* 15, no. 1 (2015): 1–19.

Kohn, Livia. "San Qing." In *The Encyclopedia of Taoism*, edited by Fabrizio Pregadio, 840–44. London: Routledge, 2008.

Kuhn, Philip A. *Chinese among Others: Emigration in Modern Times.* Lanham, MD: Rowman & Littlefield, 2009.

Lamb, Alistair. *Mandarin Road to Old Hué: Narratives of Anglo-Vietnamese Diplomacy from the 17th Century to the Eve of French Conquest.* Hamden: Archon Books, 1970.

Leroux, Ernest, ed. *Recueil d'itinéraires et de voyages dans l'Asie Centrale et l'Extrême Orient.* Paris: Librarie de la Société Asiatique de Paris, de l'Ecole de Langues Orientales vivantes, 1878.

Li, Tana. "Between Mountains and the Sea: Trades in Early Nineteenth-Century Northern Vietnam." *Journal of Vietnamese Studies* 7, no. 2 (2012): 68–86.

Li Zhijun 李智君. *Fengxia zhi hai: Mingqing Zhongguo Minnan haiyang dili yanjiu* 風下之海：明清中國閩南海洋地理研究. Beijing: Commercial Press, 2021.

Lin Jiahui 林佳慧. "Cai Tinglan *Hainan zazhu* yanjiu 蔡廷蘭《海南雜著》研究. Master's thesis, National Chung Hsing University, 2011.

Lin Shuhui 林淑慧. "Lüyou, jiyi yu lunshu: Cai Tinglan *Hainan zazhu* de kuajie zhi lü 旅遊、記憶與論述—蔡廷蘭《海南雜著》的跨界之旅." *Hanxue yanjiu*, no. 4 (2008): 219–47.

Liu Haifeng 劉海峰. "Taiwan juren zai Fujian xiangshi zhong de biaoxian 台灣舉人在福建鄉試中的表現." *Xiamen Daxue xuebao*, no. 6 (2013).

Macauley, Melissa. *Distant Shores: Colonial Encounters on China's Maritime Frontier.* Princeton, NJ: Princeton University Press, 2021.

Matisoff, James. "Sino-Tibetan Linguistics: Present State and Future Prospects." *Annual Review of Anthropology* 20 (1991): 69–504.

Miles, Steven B. "Strange Encounters on the Cantonese Frontier: Region and Gender in Kuang Lu's (1604–1650) *Chiya.*" *Nan Nu: Men, Women & Gender in Early and Imperial China* 8, no. 1 (2006): 115–55.

———. *Upriver Journeys: Diaspora and Empire in Southern China, 1570–1850.* Cambridge, MA: Harvard Asia Center, 2017.

Millward, James. "We Need a New Approach to Teaching Modern Chinese History: We Have Lazily Repeated False Narratives for Too Long." Review of *Making China Modern: From the Great Qing to Xi Jinping*, by Klaus Mühlhahn. *James Millward* (blog). *Medium.com*, October 8, 2020. https://

jimmillward.medium.com/we-need-a-new-approach-to-teaching-modern
-chinese-history-we-have-lazily-repeated-false-d24983bd7ef2.

Miyazaki Ichisada 宮崎市定. *Kakyo* 科挙. Ōsaka: Akitaya, 1946.

Morrison, Robert. *A Dictionary of the Chinese Language.* Macao: East India
Company's Pr., 1822.

Murray, Dian H. *Pirates of the South China Coast, 1790–1810.* Stanford, CA:
Stanford University Press, 1987.

Ngô Đức Thọ, Nguyễn Thuý Nga, and Nguyễn Hữu Múi, eds. *Các Nhà Khoa
Bảng Việt Nam (1075–1919)* [Inventory of Vietnamese degree holders,
1075–1919]. Hà Nội: Nhà Xuất Bản Văn Học, 2006.

Ngô Đức Thọ and Emmanuel Poisson, trans. *Nghiên Cứu Chữ Húy Việt Nam
qua Các Triều Đại* [Forbidden characters in Vietnam throughout history].
Hà Nội: Văn Hóa, 1997.

Norman, Jerry. "The Mĭn Dialects in Historical Perspective." *Journal of Chinese
Linguistics Monograph Series,* no. 3 (1991): 323–58.

Phú Bình. "Tứ Bàn từ 'man' đến 'chợ,'" *Đất và Người Xứ Quảng,* May 20, 2018.
http://baoquangnam.vn/dat-va-nguoi-xu-quang/201805/tu-ban-tu-man-
den-cho-795234/.

Phung, Hieu M. "Land & Water: A History of Fifteenth-Century Vietnam from
an Environmental Perspective." PhD diss., University of Hawai'i, 2017.

Po, Ronald. *The Blue Frontier: Maritime Vision and Power in the Qing Empire.*
Cambridge, UK: Cambridge University Press, 2018.

Pollack, Sheldon. *The Language of the Gods in the World of Men: Sanskrit, Culture and Power in Premodern India.* Berkeley: University of California Press,
2006.

Pomeranz, Kenneth. *The Great Divergence: China, Europe, and the Making of the
Modern World Economy.* Princeton, NJ: Princeton University Press, 2000.

Pore, William F. "The Inquiring Literatus: Yi Sugwang's 'Brush-Talks' with
Phùng Khắc Khoan in Beijing in 1598." *Transactions of the Royal Asiatic Society—Korea Branch* 83 (2008): 1–26.

Preston, Ken. "The Use of Basketry in the Hulls of Vietnamese Seagoing
Boats. The Status as of 2015 and the Question of the Future." *Moussons: Re-
cherche en sciences humaines sur l'Asie du Sud-Est* 27 (2016): 23–58.

Pulleyblank, Edwin G. *Outline of Classical Chinese Grammar.* Vancouver: University of British Columbia Press, 1995.

Qiu Puyan 邱普艷. "Yuenan Huaqiao shehui de xingcheng yu fazhan 越南華僑
社會的形成與發展." *Dongnanya Nanya yanjiu,* no. 1 (2012): 82–87.

Reid, Anthony. "Chinese Trade and Southeast Asian Economic Expansion in the Later Eighteenth and Early Nineteenth Centuries: An Overview." In Cooke and Li, *Water Frontier*, 21–34.

Roberts, Edmund. *Embassy to the Eastern Courts of Cochin-China, Siam, and Muscat, in the US Sloop of War Peacock, during the years 1832–3–4*. New York, 1837.

Sima Qian 司馬遷. *Shiji* 史記. Beijing: Zhonghua, 1963.

Simmons, Richard VanNess. "Whence Came Mandarin? Qīng Guānhuà, the Běijīng Dialect, and the National Language Standard in Early Republican China." *Journal of the American Oriental Society* 137, no. 1 (2017): 63–88.

Staunton, George. *An Authentic Account of an Embassy from the King of Great Britain to the Emperor of China*. London: W. Bulmer and Co., 1797.

Su Shi 蘇軾. *Su Shi shiji* 蘇軾詩集. Beijing: Zhonghua, 1982, 43:2366.

Su Zhe 蘇轍. *Su Zhe ji* 蘇轍集.Vol. 3. Edited by Zeng Zaozhuang 曾棗莊. Beijing, Yuwen, 60:29.

Tang Xiyong 湯熙勇. "Chuannan yu haiwai lixian jingyan: Yi Cai Tinglan piaoliu Yuenan wei zhongxin 船難與海外歷險經驗——以蔡廷蘭漂流越南為中心." *Renwen ji shehuikexue jikan*, no. 9 (2009): 480–93.

Taylor, Keith W. *History of the Vietnamese*. Cambridge, UK: Cambridge University Press, 2013.

Teng Lanhua 滕蘭花 and He Zhe 何哲. "*Yuenan youli ji* zhong suojian de Yuenan Beiqi Huaqiao Huaren tanxi 《越南遊歷記》中所見的越南北圻華僑華人探析." *Bagui qiaokan*, no. 3 (2016).

Trần Ích Nguyên (陳益源). *Thái Đình Lan & tác phẩm Hải Nam Tạp Trứ*. Translated by Ngô Đức Thọ and Hoàng Văn Lâ. Hà Nội: Nhà Xuất Bản Lao Động, 2009.

Trần Quang Đức. *Ngàn Năm Áo Mũ: Lịch Sử Trang Phục Việt Nam Giai Đoạn 1009–1945* [A thousand years of caps and robes]. Hà Nội: Nhã Nam & Thế Giới, 2013.

Trịnh, Khắc Mạnh, Văn Nguyên Nguyễn, and Philippe Papin. *Tổng Tập Thác Bản Văn Khắc Hán Nôm = Corpus des Inscriptions Anciennes Du Việt-Nam = Corpus of Ancient Vietnamese Inscriptions*. Hà Nội: Nhà xuất bản Văn hóa-thông tin, 2005.

Vũ Đường Luân. "The Politics of Frontier Mining: Local Chieftains, Chinese Miners, and Upland Society in the Nông Văn Vân Uprising in the Sino-Vietnamese Border Area (1833–1835). *Cross-Currents: East Asian History and Culture Review*, no. 11 (June 2014): 31–58.

Vũ Đường Luân and Tana Li. "Chinese Merchants and Mariners in Nineteenth-Century Tongking." In Cooke, Li, and Anderson *The Tongking Gulf through History*, 143–160.

Vu Hướng Đông and Đinh Văn Minh. "Vài nét về tác giả và văn bản Hải Nam tạp trứ." *Tạp chí Hán Nôm*, no. 5 (84) 2007: 63–72.

Wang Dezhao 王德昭. "Qingdai de keju rushi yu zhengfu 清代的科舉入仕與政府." *Zhongguo Wenhua Yanjiusuo xuebao* 12 (1981).

Wang Gungwu. *The Chinese Overseas: From Earthbound China to the Quest for Autonomy.* Cambridge, MA: Harvard University Press, 2000.

———. "Merchants without Empire: The Hokkien Sojourning Communities." In *The Rise of the Merchant Empires: Long Distance Trade in the Early Modern World, 1350–1750*, edited by James D. Tracy, 400–403. Cambridge, UK: Cambridge University Press, 1990.

———. "Sojourning: The Chinese Experience in Southeast Asia." In *Sojourners and Settlers: Histories of Southeast Asia and the Chinese*, edited by Anthony Reid, 1–14. Honolulu: University of Hawai'i Press, 2001.

Wheeler, Charles. "Interests, Institutions, and Identity: Strategic Adaptation and the Ethni-evolution of *Minh Hương* (Central Vietnam), 16th–19th Centuries." *Itinerario* 39, no. 1 (2015): 141–66.

———. "An Offshore Perspective on Vietnamese Zen." In *Asia Inside Out: Changing Times*, edited by Eric Tagliacozzo, Helen F. Siu, and Peter C. Perdue, 135–62. Cambridge, MA: Harvard University Press, 2015.

———. "Placing the 'Chinese Pirates' of the Gulf of Tongking at the End of the Eighteenth Century." In *Asia Inside Out: Connected Places*, edited by Eric Tagliacozzo, Helen F. Siu, and Peter C. Perdue, 30–63. Cambridge, MA: Harvard University Press, 2015.

White, John. *History of a Voyage to the China Sea.* Boston: Wells and Lilly, 1823.

Wickberg, Edgar. *The Chinese in Philippine Life, 1850–1898.* New Haven, CT: Yale University Press, 1965.

Woodside, Alexander Barton. *Vietnam and the Chinese Model.* Cambridge, MA: Harvard Asia Center, 1971.

Xu Feng'en 許奉恩. *Licheng* 里乘. Ji'nan: Qilu Shushe, 2004.

Yamaguchi Kaname 山口要. "19 shiji Hanyu guanhua yinxi yanjiu" 19世紀漢語官話音系研究. PhD diss., Kumamoto Gakuen University, 2013.

You Jianshe 尤建設. "17 shiji houqi-19 shiji zhongqi Yuenan de huaqiao huaren 17世紀後期-19世紀中期越南的華僑華人." Master's thesis, Zhengzhou University, 2003.

Yu Xiangdong 于向東. "*Hainan zazhu* de zuozhe yu banben" 《海南雜著》的作者與版本, *Dongnanya yanjiu*, no. 4 (2007).

Zhang Baichun. "The Introduction of European Astronomical Instruments and the Related Technology into China during the Seventeenth Century." *EASTM* 20 (2003): 99–131.

Zhang Weidong 張衛東. "Shilun jindai nanfang Guanhua de xingcheng jiqi diwei 試論近代南方官話的形成及其地位." *Shenzhen Daxue xuebao* 15, no. 3 (1998).

Zhao Rushi 趙汝適. *Zhufan zhi* 諸蕃志. Taipei: Taiwan Yinhang jingji yanjiushi, 1961

Zhongguo Shehui Kexueyuan Yuyan Yanjiusuo 中國社會科學院語言研究所, Zhongguo Shehui Kexueyuan Minzuxue Yu Renleixue Yanjiusuo 中國社會科學院民族學與人類學研究所, and Xianggang Chengshi Daxue Yuyan Zixunkexue Yanjiu Zhongxin 香港城市大學語言資訊科學研究中心, eds. *Zhongguo yuyan ditu ji: Hanyu fangyan juan* 中國語言地圖集：漢語方言卷. 2nd ed. Beijing: Commercial Press, 2012.

Zhou Changji 周長楫, ed., *Minnan fangyan dacidian* 閩南方言大詞典. Fuzhou: Fujian Renmin, 2006.

Zhu Yunying 朱云影. *Zhongguo wenhua dui Ri Han Yue de yingxiang* 中國文化對日韓越的影響. Guilin: Guangxi Shifan Daxue, 2007.

INDEX

Page numbers in *italics* refer to illustrations and maps.
Miscellany refers to *Miscellany of the South Seas*.

Fujian Province: Hokkien as language of southeastern, 9; map of coast, 4; Minh Hương roots in, 19; native-place lodge, 22, 92; provincial exams taken by Cai in, 7; *tulou* communal houses, 108, 156n68; Zhao Shenzhen as governor general of, 107, 155–56n67; Zhu Xi celebrated as a native of, 108–9, 156n69. *See also* Fuzhou; Hokkien; Longxi (in Fujian); Zhangzhou Prefecture; Zhao'an County (Fujian)

Fujianese people: Cai's interactions with, from Longxi, 29, 73–74, 104; Cai's interactions with, from Tong'an, 9, 29, 71, 75, 76, 86, 88, 92; financial support for Cai's return to China, 90

Fuzhou: Chinese migrant families from, 30, 90; dialect of Hokkien spoken in, 145n45; location of, 4; native-place association, 22; provincial exams taken by Cai in, 7; as separate from Fujian Province in Qing China, 145n45; typhoon encountered en route from, 1, 7

Ghost Gate (Quý Môn Quan), 57, 94, 154n48

gifts and gift exchange: Cai's comfort with, 35; Cai's poetry as, 84, 87; Euro-American misunderstanding of, 34–35; financial support for Cai's return to China, 90–91, 94; for officials in markets, 124; presentation on copper trays, 35, 57, 67, 68, 123; resources gifted to Cai to return home, 73, 75, 77, 88, 100, 127

Gotō Hitoshi, 15

gu poison, 89

Guangdong Province: financial support for Cai's return to China, 90; location of, 4, 11; native-place associations, 9; Qiongzhou under the jurisdiction of, 51, 149n2; shrine to Duke Wen of Han in, 107

Guangzhou: Cai's travels from Goat City to Laolong, Guangdong, 107; native-place association, 22; location of, 6, 11

Guanxi (or Xiaoxi): Cai's visit to, 108; location of, 11

Gui Xifu, *Traelogue of the Renxu Year* compared with, 109

Hà Nội (Hanoi): Lê palace visited by Cai, 92; "nha tử" ships in, 125; other names for, 38–39, 92, 114, 156n2, 157n19

Hà Tiên, overseas Chinese community in, 25

Hai Bà Trưng temple, 93. *See also* Trưng sisters

Hainan Island. *See* Qiongzhou

Hainan zazhu (*Miscellany of the South Seas*), publication in 1837, 1; meaning of title, 41–42

hairstyle, queue, 14, 21, 70–71

Hakka (Kejia/Khách gia): native-place association, 22, 145n45; and Pun Tao Kung, 36

Hargett, James M., 153n39

He Xianwen (or Hà Hiế Văn), 38, 114, 148n87, 157n17

Hồ Bảo Định, 30, 90

Hồ Đê (Hồ Hán Thương), 112, 156n5

Hồ dynasty, Tây Kinh ("western capital") in Thanh Hóa, 10, 156

Ông Ích Khiêm, 91, 153n40

overseas Chinese: ancient customs followed by, 121; Bản Đầu Công worshipped by, 36; Cai's return to China financially supported by, 90–91, 94; interactions with Cai in Vietnam, 28–30, 89–90, 92–94; maritime settlements compared with colonies, 25–26. *See also* merchants, Chinese; Minh Hương; native-place associations (*bang*); Tang people (Tangren/Đường nhân)

Paracel Islands, *6*, *10*, 16–17, 19

peacocks: marketed in Vietnam according to Cai, 126; peacock-pheasants observed by Cai, 36, 90, 95, 153n39; Suhe birds in Annam, 126–27

Penghu Islands (or Pescadores Islands): Cai Tinglan as a native of, 2–3, 47; hurricanes and storms in the Penghu region, 144n13; location in the Taiwan Strait, 3, *4*, *6*, *11*, 47; as a subprefecture of Fujian province, 143n4

Phan Thanh Giản, 28, 76–77, 152n17

pheasants. *See* peacocks

Phú Xuân [Huế, popularly called Thuận Hóa]: Cai's visit to, 35–36, 81–84; cannons in, *85*; city walls, 81, *82*, 152n25; Imperial College in, 87, 153n31; location of, *10*; occupied by Nguyễn Quang Trung, 113; palaces described by Cai, 83–84, *84*

pillars, marking southern border of Han empire, 95, 111, 154n51

pirates: Chinese, employed by the Tây Sơn, 38; He Xianwen, 38, 114, 148n87, 157n17; in Nguyễn dynasty annals, 1

platform daybed (*ta*), 35, 68, 71, 86

Po, Ronald, 17–18

Pollock, Sheldon, 27

Pomeranz, Kenneth, 24

Pun Tao Kung, 36

Qing dynasty: civil service examinations, 3–4; and inner and outer sea, 17–18

—Daoguang: Cai's return from Vietnam, 47, 51, 61; Cai's studies with Zhou Kai, 47; Nông Văn Vân rebellion, 39, 97, 115–16

—Jiaqing reign, 113

—Qianlong reign, 113

Qiongzhou (Hainan Island): under jurisdiction of Guangdong Province, 51, 149n2; location of, *6*, *10*, 17; native-place association,

Qu Yuan (Lingjun), 129, 159n2

Quảng Bình Province (or Đồng Hới): Cai's visit to, 86–88; location of, *10*

Quảng Nam Province: Hội An market town in, 43, 76, 124; location of, *10*; Tây Kinh mistakenly placed in, by Cai, 111, 156n2

Quảng Ngãi Province: market town in, 43. *See also* Thời Cẩn (Sa Cẩn) station

Quang Trung. *See* Tây Sơn dynasty— Nguyễn Quang Trung (or Nguyễn Huệ)

queue hairstyle, 14, 21, 70–71

Quy Nhơn, 157n11, 157n16

"Record of Peril on the High Seas," 61–66; Xiong Yiben's description of, 129; Zhou Yungao's commentary, 66

trade: Chinese networks and Nguyễn economy, 25; market towns (*phố*), 43; private export of certain commodities banned, 125; unlawful activity confronted by the Nguyễn, 28, 146n56; Vietnam and maritime Chaozhou connection detailed in *Miscellany*, 26. *See also* merchants

for Trần Cảo to be made king, 112;
Liu Hong'ao on, 53; on marriage
customs, 120, 122; "wheels" (sedan
chairs) described, 118, 158n26; Xiong
Yiben on, 129, 130; Zhou Kaizhong
on, 53; Zhou Yungao on, 127
Vietnamese merchants. *See* merchants,
Vietnamese
Vĩnh Long, 126, 153n35
Vũ Đường Luân, on *phở*, 43
Vũ Văn Dũng, 114, 157n15

Wang Bo (Wang Zian), 129, 159n2
Wang Gungwu, 145n38
Wheeler, Charles, 17, 148n87
White, John, 16, 147–48n74, 150n1,
150n3, 158n26
Wickberg, Edgar, 36
women: customs regarding, 121–22;
laws regarding, 120; as performers,
123–24; as porters, 108; spirits, 77
Woodside, Alexander Barton, 5, 151n14,
152n29

Xiamen (Heron Island): location of, *4*,
11; provincial exams taken by Cai in,
47, 51, 61
Xiong Yiben, postscript by, 129–30
Xu Feng'en, *Licheng*, 159n39
Xu Xiake, 13

Ye Xianggao, *Cerulean Cloud Collection*,
131, 132
Yue, as a term for Guangdong, 71

Zhangzhou Prefecture: Cai's interactions with a Fujianese from, 94;
dialect of Hokkien spoken in, 29;
location of, *4, 6, 11*; mountainous
region described by Cai, 108
Zhao'an County (Fujian): Cai's interactions with natives from, 89; dialect
of Hokkien spoken in, 29; Sim Liang as a native of, 30, 31, 67, 76
Zhaoqing Prefecture: Cai's exploration
for traces of Zhu Xi, 108–9; Guangzhou native-place association, 22;
location of, *11*
Zhao Shenzhen, 107, 155–56n67
Zhou Kai (circuit intendent): Cai's
concerns about famine in Penghu
brought to, 12, 47; preface by, 47–49
Zhou Yungao (circuit intendent): as
circuit intendant at Xiamen, 61; on
"Record of Peril on the High Seas,"
66; Trần Văn Trung's memory of
meeting, in Xiamen, 96; on "Travelogue of the Fiery Wasteland," 109;
on "Vietnam Chronicle," 127; wait
for Cai's return, 55
Zhu Xi, 108–9

44396651R00113